W9-DEV-868

THE DEMISE OF THE DOLLAR . . .

AND WHY IT'S EVEN BETTER FOR YOUR INVESTMENTS

THE DEMISE OF THE DOLLAR . . .

AND WHY IT'S EVEN BETTER FOR YOUR INVESTMENTS

Revised and Updated

ADDISON WIGGIN

Foreword by Chuck Butler

WILEY

John Wiley & Sons, Inc.

Copyright © 2005, 2008 by Addison Wiggin. All rights reserved.

Published by John Wiley & Sons, Inc., Hoboken, New Jersey.
Published simultaneously in Canada.

No part of this publication may be reproduced, stored in a retrieval system, or trans-
mitted in any form or by any means, electronic, mechanical, photocopying, recording,
scanning, or otherwise, except as permitted under Section 107 or 108 of the 1976
United States Copyright Act, without either the prior written permission of the
Publisher, or authorization through payment of the appropriate per-copy fee to the
Copyright Clearance Center, Inc., 222 Rosewood Drive, Danvers, MA 01923,
(978) 750-8400, fax (978) 646-8600, or on the web at www.copyright.com. Requests
to the Publisher for permission should be addressed to the Permissions Department,
John Wiley & Sons, Inc., 111 River Street, Hoboken, NJ 07030, (201) 748-6011,
fax (201) 748-6008, or online at http://www.wiley.com/go/permissions.

Limit of Liability/Disclaimer of Warranty: While the publisher and author have
used their best efforts in preparing this book, they make no representations or
warranties with respect to the accuracy or completeness of the contents of this book
and specifically disclaim any implied warranties of merchantability or fitness for a
particular purpose. No warranty may be created or extended by sales representatives
or written sales materials. The advice and strategies contained herein may not
be suitable for your situation. You should consult with a professional where
appropriate. Neither the publisher nor author shall be liable for any loss of profit
or any other commercial damages, including but not limited to special, incidental,
consequential, or other damages.

For general information on our other products and services or for technical
support, please contact our Customer Care Department within the United States at
(800) 762-2974, outside the United States at (317) 572-3993 or fax (317) 572-4002.

Wiley also publishes its books in a variety of electronic formats. Some content that
appears in print may not be available in electronic books. For more information
about Wiley products, visit our web site at www.wiley.com.

ISBN 978-0-470-28724-8

Printed in the United States of America.

10 9 8 7 6 5 4 3 2 1

CONTENTS

FOREWORD

It had been two years since I first read *The Demise of the Dollar* when Addison approached me to write a forward for the revised version. A circling back to refresh my memory was in order.

Since the original release of *The Demise of the Dollar,* 2005, the dollar has continued its long ride down the slippery slope. *Demise of the Dollar* clearly demonstrated the reasons for this dollar to remain weak, and this revised version brings you up to date.

The mantra of the current administration rings empty when they talk about "a strong dollar being in the best interests of the U.S." The dollar has lost another third of its value against the euro since the administration first uttered those words. And recently Fed chairman Bernanke suggested that the dollar's weakness was not a concern to the Fed.

So, whose concern is it? U.S. Treasury Secretary Henry Paulson tells us that he believes in the strong dollar policy, while at the same time reprimanding China for allowing a weak currency. How can Paulson say he believes in a strong dollar when he wants the Chinese renminbi to appreciate against the dollar? When cornered, Paulson has been heard to say that currency values should be set in a competitive marketplace based on underlying economic fundamentals. So, a look at economic fundamentals is what we need to do, and in the *The Demise of the Dollar,* you will find plenty of fodder to bring you to the conclusion that the demise of the dollar is more of a reality in 2007 than ever before!

Today, the U.S. current account deficit requires $3 billion a day in foreign financing. How long can we continue to count on the kindness of strangers? In 2005, our trade deficit was $600 billion and growing. Today, we run a trade deficit of $710 billion per year, and it's still growing.

U.S. consumers continue to spend money they don't really have, or should be saving. The net savings rate in the United States has turned negative, and wages in the United States have continually fallen for years. The fundamentals for a recovery of the dollar do not look like those associated with a strong currency.

And money supply? Well, the government no longer prints M3. As a guide, we no longer know how many dollars "Helicopter Ben Bernanke" now prints on his printing press. But one thing we know for sure is that money supply is abundant, and therefore inflation remains unchecked in the United States. Now we've entered a new rate cutting cycle, as the Fed turns its back on inflation.

The credit-based economy and liberal monetary policies of the Fed allowed inflation to remain low for years, but slowly, and predictably, inflation pressures increased, and today inflation, like money supply, is abundant in our economy.

So, here we sit with the biggest fiat currency of all time, teetering on the brink of disaster, and only a few will tell you the truth about the dollar.

In *The Demise of the Dollar,* you will find economic theory that tells you why all of these awful things are happening to our economy and dollar. It will be one of the most well-written economics books you've ever read. Economic books can border on dry and boring, but this one is educational, informative, and very accessible to the average Joe who needs protection from our misguided Fed and governmental policies and misinformation campaigns.

Once again Addison Wiggin has knocked the cover off the ball with his *The Demise of the Dollar*!

—Chuck Butler

THE DEMISE OF THE DOLLAR . . .

AND WHY IT'S EVEN BETTER FOR YOUR INVESTMENTS

INTRODUCTION

FALL OF THE GREAT DOLLAR STANDARD

According to the press, the world's prettiest face, Gisele Bündchen, wants to be paid in euros for U.S. modeling gigs, and in his new video, the rapper Jay-Z triumphantly holds euros—not dollars—in his upraised fist. The day after Thanksgiving 2007, anxious retailers started opening their doors before dawn to draw shoppers. Overseas visitors, meanwhile, are packing the streets of New York City, scooping up bargains. "I just saved $2,000 on this Rolex," said one shopper from Great Britain, waving her new watch at a reporter's camera. And no one's laughing now at the Canadian loonie, which reached parity with the U.S. dollar in September 2007—for the first time since 1976.

Pretty faces, angry rappers, desperate U.S. retailers, happy shopaholic tourists, and Canadians who have finally turned the tables on us . . . what on earth is happening as 2007 draws to a close and this new edition of *The Demise of the Dollar* goes to press?

Although Gisele has denied making any such claim about her payment currency of preference (and has stated that she is happy to earn salaries in a variety of currencies), the fact that this story spread like wildfire through media outlets from Bloomberg and CNBC to E! News and *People* speaks volumes. The dollar has little cred(ibility) on the streets of New York—or pretty much on any street around the world. The twilight of the Great Dollar Standard Era is upon us. The euro is now worth almost 50 percent more than the U.S. dollar, and in Great Britain, you can get two U.S. dollars for every British pound.

In 2007, the famous refrain in the poem by Emma Lazarus describing the flood of foreigners streaming to U.S. shores needs to be updated to "Give me your tired, your rich, your huddled masses yearning to shop free." Seven out of every $10 that fuels our gross domestic product (GDP), the measure of a nation's productivity and hence security, comes—not from goods and services that we produce and sell—but from shopping. We're addicted to cheap credit.

Alan Greenspan, the longtime chairman of the Federal Reserve, set us on this runaway course, and Ben Bernanke, the new chairman since February 2006, is steadily following in his footsteps. In late October, he voted with the rest of Federal Open Market Committee (FOMC), the Fed's policy-making arm, to cut interest rates for the third month in a row this year. He is not the "un-Greenspan," as the financial press called him early in his tenure; he is the reincarnation of Mr. Irrational Exuberance himself, and he's pushing the same old monetary policy: "In debt? No problem. Spend more money—we'll print it for you."

In his autography, *The Age of Turbulence,* released by Penguin Press in September 2007—ironically, a few days before the second rate cut of the year—Greenspan says he thought it was wrong to increase scrutiny of subprime mortgages. Call me cynical, but increased scrutiny might have helped; 52 percent of these risky mortgages, made to borrowers with poor credit histories, were originated by companies and organizations with zero federal supervision. "I really didn't get it until very late in 2005 and 2006," Greenspan told Reuters in an interview, apologizing for the housing bubble he helped create, which led to the subprime mortgage mess and the credit crisis.

In the third and fourth quarters of 2007, Citigroup ($11.38 billion), Merrill Lynch ($8.48 billion), Morgan Stanley ($4.68 billion), and Barclays ($2.7 billion) led the pack in write-downs—government-approved losses on these loans. In the fourth quarter alone, we're looking at a staggering $44 billion.

And the fallout isn't over yet. In October, the U.S. Commerce Department reported that housing permits fell to a 14-year low, the lowest seasonally adjusted level since July 1993. In distressed markets such as San Francisco, home builders are shaving off as much as $150,000 from prices. And foreclosures nearly doubled (94 percent) from October 2006 to October 2007. "We have not seen a nation-wide decline in housing like this since the Great Depression," said Wells Fargo chief executive John Stumpf, who thinks we're in for more rough play in 2008. "I don't think we're in the ninth inning of unwinding this. If we are, it's going to be an extra-inning game."

Well, he was right, unfortunately. By the time the year wound down, sales of new homes had plummeted 26.4 percent, according to the U.S. Department of Commerce—the worst slump since 1980. And housing starts fell almost as hard, by 24.8 percent.

Business Week summed up the state of the nation with my favorite headline of 2007: "The Economy on the Edge."

Is there any good news? You bet! There are steps that smart investors can take now to escape from their vulnerability to the dollar's inevitable fall. This book lays out the problem and explains how we got here. It also explains how, with a properly positioned portfolio, the demise of the dollar could actually be beneficial to your financial outlook.

But first, let's start with a little history lesson so we can understand why we're facing a dead end with the U.S. dollar, which once set the monetary standard around the world.

It was tantamount to an international margin call—and even the most unsophisticated investor can guess that the words *margin call* don't bring good news. Your broker calls to tell you that your securities—which you bought with borrowed money—are in trouble, and you've got two choices, which really amount to no choice at all: either deposit more money (which you don't have) in your account or sell off one of your assets to stay afloat. But that's exactly what then President Richard Nixon did on August 15, 1971, when he took U.S. currency off the gold standard.

Prior to 1971, in most of the world, currency had been backed by gold for more than 100 years. In the United States, dollars issued were called *silver certificates* because currency was backed by silver (or by gold in terms of purchasing power internationally).

Our system became one of *fiat money*—a system in which the government claims a value but does not back it up with gold (or other) reserves. Today, a bill of our fiat money is identified as a *Federal Reserve note*—not a certificate worth redemption in silver or gold, but literally an IOU issued by the Fed.

As we like to point out repeatedly in *The Daily Reckoning*, the gold standard was a useful and important economic tool. The fact that gold existed only in limited supply meant that it served as an inhibitor in the rapid increase of currency in circulation. The government could not simply print all the money it wanted to.

So let's look at two questions: Why did Nixon make that decision, and how has it changed everything?

THE DECLINE OF THE DOLLAR BEGINS

The official reason for going off the gold standard was to persuade U.S. trade partners to peg their currencies to the U.S. dollar; in other words, it was an attempt at getting foreign governments to realign their currency values. Why? Nixon recognized that relying on gold as settlement for international exchange of goods and services inhibited expansion of the U.S. economy.

Removing the U.S. dollar from the gold standard was an attempt at solving the problem of falling currencies overseas. The currency exchange between U.S. dollars and European and Japanese currencies was a drain on U.S. trade. This is *opposite* to the problem we face today, that of a falling dollar.

If Nixon had removed the restriction on gold value at $35 an ounce and allowed it to find its value in the open market, that would have done more to fix the international monetary problem. But removing the restriction on gold value was not considered a viable option, for two reasons:

First, it would have meant the United States was telling other countries (those with undervalued currencies) to raise their prices on exports to the United States. And that would never have gone over well in countries that, at the time, were being subsidized by the U.S. dollar, economically speaking. For example, the removal of an artificial value of gold would have required Germany to raise export prices 2.4 times above levels in effect in 1971, but at the same time, U.S. goods would continue to sell in Germany for about 41 percent of previous values.[1]

Second, the change would have drastically affected world markets of natural resources, including oil—doubling the barrel price of oil. That would not have gone over well, either—although a few years later, we did in fact experience double-digit inflation and long lines at the pump as a consequence of going off the gold standard.

THE GREAT DOLLAR STANDARD ERA

Nixon's decision was viewed as the only alternative to devaluing the dollar. Currency markets already recognized that U.S. dollars had been inflated. In December 1971, leaders of the so-called Group of Ten industrialized nations met in Washington, D.C., to officially change currency values based on the per-ounce value of gold raised from $35 to $38. The dollar was lowered 7.89 percent, while the German mark was raised 13.57 percent and the Japanese yen went up 16.9 percent.

But the abandonment of the gold standard had a far deeper and longer-lasting effect than the inflationary adjustments of the 1970s. Why? Because our "money proxy" dollar circulated based on commodity reserves (gold and silver).

Nixon was concerned that the gold standard inhibited our ability to compete with devalued currencies in other nations. The U.S. government was known to issue currency above reserves by speculating, offsetting long positions in dollars with short positions in gold, and gambling that it was unlikely that demands would be made against currency reserves. But that's exactly what happened. In the days before Nixon's decision, the British ambassador presented a demand for conversion of $3 billion in currency into gold.

If we recognize that currency is simply a form of IOU against the value of goods and services we exchange, then we can see why the tables have turned. In 1971, the major foreign currencies were devalued against the dollar *and* the gold standard.

THE FREE FALL ACCELERATES

When Nixon took the United States off the gold standard, he also tried to stabilize the economy with a series of ill-fated price controls. He wanted to curb inflation, which was increasing in 1971, a time when people actually worried about what inflation might do to their net worth. So Nixon instituted a series of wage and price controls. Listening to his Fed chairman, Arthur Burns, Nixon believed what he'd been told: that the traditional view about tight money was wrong, and the key to economic recovery was government control over prices and wages.

The belief that freezing wages and prices is an effective way to stop inflation defied economic sensibility—not to mention Nixon's Republican standards that were supposed to favor a free market. The decision to do so was part of a plan to stimulate new employment in time for the 1972 presidential election. Burns warned Nixon that going off the gold standard would be viewed in Moscow and in the Russian press—at the height of the Cold War—as a bad sign for the United States. He warned, "*Pravda* would write that this was a sign of the collapse of capitalism."[2]

While it has taken more than 30 years for the evidence to present itself fully, the decisions made by Nixon in 1971 set the process in motion. Capitalism did not collapse immediately, but it is collapsing in one important respect today. The U.S. dollar's value is falling against foreign currencies. And who is replacing the United States as the new economic world leader? China, a country that in 1971 exemplified the very worst of Communism. The misguided belief that wage and price controls would fix the economy by reducing inflation and creating new jobs was simply wrong. The decision to go off the gold standard—rather than curbing the printing of currency and taking a hit on valuation—has created a far worse problem.

Of course, the wage and price controls did not work. Yes, Nixon won reelection in 1972, but unemployment did *not* fall, and inflation did *not* go away (in fact, it got worse). The administration reimposed the freeze controls that had failed before, then quietly canceled them in April 1974, only four months before Nixon resigned. By then, unfortunately, the unavoidable expansion in inflation, unemployment, and a falling dollar had begun.

We have to remember the meaning of the gold standard, and why it served such an important role in international economic policy. The gold standard was a means by which countries agreed to fix the value of their currency, based on amounts of gold reserves. The abandonment of the gold standard during World War I when most countries involved in the fighting financed their war effort with inflationary money—IOUs—eventually contributed to the massive devaluation in the 1920s and worldwide depression of the 1930s. We should learn from history. Abandoning the gold standard devastates the world economy.

From the end of World War II until 1971, most industrialized nations adhered to the standards of the Bretton Woods system, named for the U.N. Monetary and Financial Conference held at Bretton Woods, New Hampshire, on July 22, 1944.

Several important agreements came out of that conference. The International Monetary Fund (IMF)[3] was established by the international conference to ensure regulation and order over world currencies and trade policies. This organization was a sort of worldwide version of the U.S. Federal Reserve, with power to regulate currency policies. Second, given the need for postwar reconstruction, the conference also established the International Bank for Reconstruction and Development (also known as the World Bank)[4] to provide financing to countries most devastated by World War II. Activities of these two organizations included agreement on currency controls, investment, lending activities, and foreign international activities.[5]

The Bretton Woods agreements were significant because, for the first time, there was international agreement on monetary matters—or at least the seeds of such agreements were planted. Those adhering to the gold standard recognized the value of price stability on an international basis, and it was quite visionary. While the pending end of World War II motivated much of the discussion, those in attendance also knew that future economic policy would determine the economic stability for the entire world. They knew that there were bound to be periods of inflation, unemployment, and currency instability, as part of the natural economic cycle, but the decision to go off the gold standard destroyed the orderly economic policies made possible through Bretton Woods. The period of the early 1970s was the start of a very unsettled time, based on both economic and political strife. In hindsight, it seems obvious that the decision to go off the gold standard was devastating. It didn't lead to the immediate fall of capitalism, but now—more than 30 years later—it has brought us to the precipice, and perhaps the decline, in the long-running U.S. dominance of the world economy.

THE TWILIGHT OF THE GREAT DOLLAR STANDARD ERA

American consumers face the specter of losing value in their retirement savings, finding out they cannot live on a fixed income, and suffering from chronic hyperinflation. These changes are unavoidable. Today, the problem is compounded because the U.S. dollar's value is falling. It all involves productivity changes in the United States. We have not competed with the manufacturing economies in other countries, and that is why our credit (i.e., our dollar) is suffering.

Any number of things could create a sudden, wrenching drop in the dollar's value. Consider the following three possibilities:

1. *Foreign countries drop their U.S. dollar reserves.* We depend on foreign investment in our currency to bolster its value or, at least, to slow down its fall. When that thinly held balance changes, our dollar loses its spending power. In February 2005, South Korea announced that it will stop holding U.S. dollars and bonds in its reserves—but that was only the beginning. In an odd twist of financial fate, on the same day that the Canadian loonie achieved parity with the U.S. dollar, Saudi Arabia refused to adjust rates in lockstep with the Federal Reserve. Keeping its interest rate unchanged may signal Saudi Arabia's desire to break its dollar peg. Iran, Iraq, and Kuwait have already dumped the dollar; will the Saudis be next? At a November 2007 meeting of the Organization of Petroleum Exporting Countries (OPEC)'s 13-member cartel, Iranian President Mahmoud Ahmadinejad, whose country already receives payment for 85 percent of its oil exports in nondollar currencies, urged other countries to follow suit and "designate a single hard currency aside from the U.S. dollar . . . to form the basis of our oil trade." "The empire of the dollar

has to end," chimed in Venezuela's Hugo Chavez; his state oil company changed its dollar investments to euros at his order—er, request.

Rumors are circulating that the Bank of Korea, after selling off $100 million worth of U.S. bonds in August 2007, is getting ready to sell $1 billion more, and if Washington forces trade sanctions, China, which threatened recently to cash in $900 billion of U.S. bonds, will probably follow suit. In Russia, Vladimir Putin's dream of a stock market to trade the country's natural resources in rubles is not so far-fetched; in 2005, Russia, the world's second-largest exporter of oil, followed South Korea's lead and ended the dollar peg. And once again, Sudan is hinting that it will impose trade or financial sanctions against companies that do business with the United States—only this time, the words just might have teeth.

As other countries follow suit, the dollar—and your spending power—drops. What does this mean? You will need more dollars to buy things than it takes today.

2. *Oil prices increase catastrophically.* We—and our real inflation rate—are at the mercy of Middle East oil. In 2005, we couldn't imagine what would happen if the price of oil were to double—or triple; but that's exactly what has happened in 2007 as oil kept flirting with $100-a-barrel prices. Our vulnerability is not imaginary. For example, if terrorists were to contaminate large reserves with nuclear radiation, the supply of oil would drop and prices would rise. We are all aware of our vulnerability and dependence on oil, but we don't like to think about it. Rising oil prices affect not only what you pay at the pump, but many other prices as well: nonautomotive modes of travel, the cost of utilities, and local tax rates, for example. It all adds up to unquestioned "pain at the pump" for American consumers. By September 2007, gasoline averaged $2.78 a gallon—double 2002's price. "Pain at the pump" leads to "pain in the pocketbook," as consumers know. You're not seeing double in the checkout line at the grocery store—costs really *are* double. There was a 5.6 percent increase in 2007, compared with 2.1 percent for all of 2006.

3. *The double whammy of trade and budget deficits.* We're living beyond our means. It's as simple as that, and something is going to give. The federal budget deficit—annual government spending that is higher than tax revenues—adds to the national debt at a dizzying rate, making our future interest burden higher and higher every day. Our trade deficit—bringing more things in from foreign countries than we sell to the same countries—has turned us into a nation of spendaholics. We've given up making things to sell elsewhere, closed the store, and gone shopping. But we're not spending money we have; we're *borrowing* money to spend it. In 2006, the trade and budget deficits doubled the deficits of 2001. Any head of a family knows that this cannot go on forever without the whole thing falling apart—and yet, that is precisely what we are doing on a national scale.

A SOLUTION TO YANKEE OPTIMISM

Even as our economy burns, our political leaders fiddle. They point to economic indicators to prove that our economy is strong and getting stronger. This information would be valuable . . . if only it were true.

Politicians like to measure the economy with esoteric indicators. For example, we are told that consumer confidence is up. Well, confidence is all well and good, but what if it isn't accurate? Yankee optimism has achieved a lot in the past 200 years, but it alone is not going to prevent the current dollar crisis from getting worse and worse.

Does this mean that the United States is finished? No, but it does mean that our long history of economic power and wealth is being eroded from within. For example, look at how the reality has affected you in recent years. For most people, the real state of our economy is measured in one way: *jobs.* Sure, the number of jobs rises every month, but the complete truth is not as reassuring. We are losing *high-paying* jobs in manufacturing and replacing them with *low-paying* jobs in health care, retail, and other menial job markets. Our mantra of "Yankee ingenuity can accomplish anything" is gradually being replaced with a new mantra: "Would you like fries with that?"

As manufacturing jobs continue to move to China and India, and elsewhere around the globe, you would think we'd tighten our belts. But instead, we increase our debt to spend more.

Few people, even those who consider themselves to be savvy about finance, really understand things like the trade deficit, national debt, gross domestic product, inflation, economic indicators, and the like.

The truth (one few investors want to hear) is that your local member of Congress is often just as illiterate about economics as most of us are, but the difference is that he or she has the power and position to make decisions that affect you. And he or she may be making the *wrong* decisions. You, like many other Americans, may have put aside income every month in a variety of retirement plans, long-term investments, and savings, in the belief that this is going to provide security in your old age. What are they going to be worth when you retire? Given the current state of things, you could find out that your retirement accounts are going to be worth next to nothing.

This is not the time to rush out and buy more stocks, for example, or to load up on new bargains in the property market. Quite the opposite. The subprime mess isn't over. Foreclosures keep growing. In December of 2007, we stopped believing the forecasts from the National Association of REALTORS® (NAR), which declared a market rebound in early 2008. When the NAR revised their 2007 sales forecast for existing homes the ninth consecutive month and, by our count, the tenth time that year, we officially called B.S. Making a 2007 forecast in the middle of December is lame enough. But when it's your tenth revision in 12 months, its not even fair to call it a forecast. There's an even worse slump coming as the impact of the subprime mortgage mess works its way across the landscape. By early 2009, according to Moody's Investors Service's Economy.com, estimated home prices will fall 13 percent, on average, from their 2006 peaks, but as much as 35 percent, in some markets in Florida and California.

So where should you invest? Read on. We provide you with the specifics about what's really going on with the dollar and our economy, how foreign countries ultimately control our economic fate, and how our leaders are deceiving us by telling us that we're in good shape. Finally, we offer strategies you can employ today to not only protect your financial freedom but to prosper in a dollar demise.

—Addison Wiggin
Baltimore, MD

CHAPTER 1

THE "RECOVERY" THAT WASN'T

> In all recorded history there has not been one economist who
> had to worry about where the next meal was coming from.
>
> —Peter F. Drucker

It is a modern enigma. The U.S. *dollar*—the world's reserve currency—is weakening, shrinking, falling. It has been since the inception of the Federal Reserve, the very institution assigned with the task of maintaining its value; but the decline has accelerated at an alarming rate of late.

"The dollar has slumped to new lows against other currencies" has been a refrain in the financial press for several years now. From 2000 to 2004, we scribbled out our financial insights from an office in Paris. During one 18-month period beginning in late 2002, the cost of living for those expats among us—who were paid in dollars but spent money in euros—saw their cost of living go up by almost half. In 2007, it will still cost you about 50 percent more to live or travel in Western Europe. The day before Thanksgiving 2007, the dollar fell to $1.4856 per euro—its weakest rate of exchange since the euro debuted in 1999—but it's worse for *Daily Reckoning* colleagues who work or travel in London. My colleague, Bill Bonner, spent $425 for a modest night out that included a few tickets to a West End play (the Brit equivalent of Off-Broadway), a cab ride, and dinner at a Chinese restaurant.

Still, most Americans don't ever leave the homeland, so why should we care if the dollar continues to fall in value? Well, the answer is relatively simple. Everything—milk, eggs, gas, construction supplies, you name it—now costs more—a lot more. When the Federal Reserve talks about inflation, it likes to make a distinction between overall inflation and core inflation, which excludes energy and food prices (exactly the day-to-day costs that worry most consumers).

The average price for a gallon of unleaded regular gasoline more than doubled from January 2000 to July 2006, jumping 130.5 percent, according to the U.S. Bureau of Labor Statistics, and that doesn't count the increases we've seen in 2007 that have pushed the price to $3 and more a gallon.

Inflation is even worse in grocery aisles. According to the Food Marketing Institute (FMI), the average household spends $92.50 a week on groceries—move if they have kids. In the first *six months* of 2007, grocery prices rose 7.5 percent—almost three times all of 2006's 2.1 percent increase in prices. That's the biggest annual percentage hike since 1980, according to the U.S. Department of Labor. By the time 2007 ended, food costs had swelled 5.6 percent—more than double all of 2006. Even the price of heavily regulated milk has seen a hefty jump, rising from $3 in 2001 to $3.55—and closer to $4 in some markets—by October 2007. And the upward spike continues in 2008. The U.S. Department of Agriculture is forecasting an increase of 3 to 4 percent this year.

Three dollars for a gallon of gas, mixed with falling house values—it's a double whammy for consumers. And how are they reacting? The FMI reports that meat is the most shoplifted grocery item since 2005, and as winter 2007 arrives, food pantries across the country report dwindling supplies.

What a bizarre time we live in. Economists look at the same sign and explain, "No, it doesn't cost more. They're just charging higher prices." But this is what is happening in our economy, and it is happening rapidly and all around us. Most American economists seem to not understand it (or don't want to admit it), but we're in trouble. Some economists may be finally catching up with consumers. Or maybe not. They can't seem to make up their minds. But this is the second year we've been hearing the "R" word.

In October and November 2007, the National Association for Business Economics reported that half of those economists surveyed see a recession on the horizon. But they, like the Fed, are an ever-optimistic lot: They look at the weak increase in the GDP of 2.6 percent projected from now to the fourth quarter of 2008, and pronounce it good because it is slightly ahead of 2007's anemic 2.4 percent.

Then, in November, the Fed slashed its 2008 forecasts to 1.6 to 2.5 percent, a big drop from 2.5 to 3 percent forecast earlier. Words like "subpar economic growth" and "below trend" expectations lasting into 2009 tell us what's really going on: We're headed for deep water.

We have always thought of the United States as the world's leading economic engine. If we mean this in terms of buying up goods and consuming them, the United States is no longer in the lead, and that ultimately affects our entire economy and the value of the dollar.

Now and in the near future, we will see a shift away from U.S. dominance in the economy of the world, as China becomes the new global economic engine. China buys up goods from other countries, and its rate of buying is growing by leaps and bounds.

In 2006, China's purchases of goods from abroad surged 20 percent, putting it well ahead of Japan (13 percent), the United States (11 percent), and Germany (7.32 percent). Percentages don't have the impact of dollar and yen figures, so chew on this: Midway through 2007, in May, China's trade surplus with the world widened to nearly $22.5 billion, according to U.S. Customs. That's almost $6 billion more than in April and only about a billion shy of the record. Year over year, China's exports were up 73 percent from May 2006.

These numbers are ironic, given the amount of time Treasury Secretary Henry Paulson spent with the Chinese in trade talks recently. Paulson can try to talk up the U.S. economy all he wants, but the Chinese, the numbers reflect, would rather make stuff . . . and sell it. Elsewhere in the global financial expanse, Asian markets are seeing some of their best performances in history:

- In Mumbai, the BSE Sensex topped 15,000 for the first time.
- In Tokyo, the Nikkei 225 notched a seven-year high.
- Hong Kong's market closed at a record for the fifth straight day.

- Seoul has had four consecutive record-setting days.
- In Sydney, the Aussie market marked its 34th record close this year.

Translation: Chug, chug . . . our economic engine is falling behind, weighed down by debt and too many imports.

THE GREAT GDP HOAX

Economists like to talk about recoveries in terms of jobs, consumer spending, and trade with other countries. But a lot of this is just talk. What is really happening is alarming if we look at how and where we spend money. The best way to take the temperature of the economy is by measuring what we manufacture, what we spend, what we invest, and what we buy and sell. Collectively, this is referred to as the gross domestic product (GDP).

A problem, however, is that GDP is an amalgam of different things, some of which contradict one another. So looking at GDP in total doesn't tell us what is really going on. We have to look at the trends in the different pieces that make up GDP to really understand just how dire the situation has become.

You can see how difficult it is to gain anything when you look at the usual GDP formula:

$$GDP = Consumption + Business\ investment + What\ the\ government\ spends + Exports - Imports$$

When you hear that "GDP has grown in recent years," is that good news? Not necessarily; it depends on how the components of GDP are interpreted.

The change in GDP through 2003, the most recent recession when *The Demise of the Dollar* was originally published in 2005, was skewed. While economists referred to the GDP's 2003 performance as a recovery, it didn't look at all like traditional recoveries we have seen in the past. And now we're being handed the same spin about the downturn in 2006 and the recession predicted for 2008 and beyond. We're even hearing the same rhetoric about the stimulus package. It's all similar to the talk we heard during the last recession in 2001.

In the third quarter of 2007, for example, Fed Chairman Bernanke assures us that the GDP is strong at 3.9 percent, a repeat of the second quarter's growth of 3.8 percent. But in looking at the numbers from the Bureau of Labor Statistics and at the words, in big bold letters, "GDP Grows 3.9 Percent in Third Quarter" (see the October 31, 2007, press release), it is always helpful to note the information found in the second line, in much smaller type: "Advance" estimate. The Bureau of Labor Statistics has revised the GDP down every year since 2002. A big source of real GDP growth in the third quarter of 2007 was personal consumption, which doubled from 1.4 percent in the second quarter to 3 percent. Meanwhile, housing values fell and imports grew. Does this add up to a strong GDP, in your opinion?

So far this year, inflation has risen 3.6 percent—a full percentage point above inflation in all of 2006 of 2.5 percent. That says a lot about reliable government numbers. If we depend on the government to give us the information we rely on, it would be nice to get realistic information and not just answers they think we want to hear. The latest recovery isn't really a recovery at all—in spite of what we are told by those in power.

Economists also like to point out *surges,* those signs that the recovery is strong. For example, we were told that in the third quarter of 2003 GDP surged 8.2 percent—proof of a strong recovery. But it wasn't really a surge at all, only a one-time burst in consumer spending driven by tax rebates and the mortgage refinancing bubble.

While economists like momentum and surges, they hate bubbles. These are fake trends, false surges, and aberrations that don't have any momentum at all. So when we recognize that the growth in GDP was caused by an obvious bubble, it destroys the argument. Maybe GDP didn't really surge at all. Maybe it fell when we take reality into account.

In 2003 (and for good reason), we experienced the country's slowest economic recovery ever after a recession, and it doesn't look any better in 2007. We have gone through a strange period where several conditions were combined: record-low interest rates, an exploding budget deficit, record-high consumer debt, and the mess in the credit markets, which created the mortgage meltdown that has led to the decline in housing values. This affects the value of our dollar because, in the big scheme of things, the fact that we import far more than we export—the trade deficit—is a huge problem that will ultimately destroy the U.S. dollar and its spending power.

Combined with the government budget deficit, we are faced with a double-play threat to the dollar's value. The huge trade and budget deficits (known in economic circles as the current account deficit) are the real indicators we should be watching, not the net GDP.

In April 2007, the U.S. trade deficit was more than twice as big as China's surplus—$58.5 billion. That says a lot about the state of our economy. We even set a record: From 2001 to 2006, we more than doubled our deficit, from $365 billion to now $763 billion.

To make matters worse, in September, Congress raised the ceiling on debt by $850 billion, to $9.815 trillion, to accommodate our growing girth. Yes, I said *trillion*. We came close to overreaching the $9 trillion mark ($8.993 trillion) in 2007, which is why Congress had to raise the ceiling. That's the third time since the end of fiscal year 2003 that Congress has taken this action, but that doesn't seem to bother anyone else but me and David Walker, former head of the GAO, now president and CEO of the newly founded Peter G. Peterson Foundation. Walker, who has been auditing the federal debt since 1997, noted these startling facts in the letter prefacing the most recent audit:

> We have audited the Schedule of Federal Debt since fiscal year 1997. Over this period, total federal debt has increased by 73 percent. During the last 4 fiscal years, managing the federal debt has continued to be a challenge as evidenced by the growth of total federal debt by $2,210 billion, or 33 percent, from $6,793 billion as of September 30, 2003, to $8,993 billion as of September 30, 2007.[1]

True, the budget deficit has slowed down in each of the past three years, from $248 billion in 2006 to $163 billion in 2007. But that's still a heck of a lot of money, and it's not the worst of the problem, says Walker:

> . . . our nation's real challenge is not short-term deficits, rather it's the U.S. government's impending longer-term structural deficits and related debt burdens. Indeed, what we call the longer-term fiscal challenge is not in the distant future. The first of the baby boomers became eligible for early retirement under Social Security on January 1, 2008 . . . and for Medicare benefits just 3 years later. . . .

GAO's long-range fiscal policy simulations show that the nation's current fiscal condition is but a prelude to a much more daunting long-term fiscal challenge.[2]

Is anyone listening to this guy? If you want to read more, see "Our Nation's Fiscal Outlook: The Federal Government's Long-Term Budget Imbalance," available at www.gao.gov/special.pubs/longterm.[3]

In spite of the misplaced boasts to the contrary, we need to evaluate economic news from a realistic point of view. In order to judge whether something is good or bad, it needs a reasonable measure. The way American statisticians measure the economy deludes us about the extent of America's dollar problem.

Normally, in a downturn in the economy, people take stock of their personal balance sheets, pare back, pay off a little debt, and get their ducks in a row. Not so in 2001, 2006, and, if the history of our habits proves true, in 2008. Americans pull out their credit cards and continue to spend their way right through a recession—so much so that the real work that generally takes place in a recession never happens. Debts don't get paid off. Bad loans don't get written off. The recession never really happened—that's what we believe.

But we have kept ourselves in the dark, convinced that the economic recovery is strong because "they" have told us so. Realistically, we remain in the dark. Real GDP declined just 0.6 percent in 2001, well below the average 2 percent decline of previous postwar recessions. The great question, of course, is: What actually made this recession so mild? Quoting then chairman of the Federal Reserve, Alan Greenspan: "The mildness and brevity of the downturn are a testament to the notable improvement in the resilience and flexibility of the U.S. economy."[4]

This position—that the U.S. economy is *resilient* or *flexible*—is a widespread view among American economists. It needs drastic revision because, well, the assumption itself is absolutely false. The 2001 recession *was* unusually mild, but this positive sign was more than offset by exceptionally weak economic growth in the two years following the recession—and they don't like to talk about that.

In the case of the elusive and misleading (but favorite) indicator, the GDP, the decline in all postwar recessions has averaged 2 percent. But this average loss has always been followed by vigorous recoveries. On average, over the three years of recession and recovery, there is typically an average net GDP growth of 8.2 percent. Now let's compare: Over the three years 2001–2003, covering recession and recovery, real GDP grew only 5.7 percent.

So any boast about a particularly mild recession, not to mention our economy's extraordinary resilience and flexibility, is an exaggeration.

This talk about the economy's resilience and flexibility is inaccurate for still another reason. Recessions were always periods of sharply slower debt growth and repayment, reflecting retrenchment in spending. The 2001 recession, in contrast, was a period when debt growth accelerated, and that is precisely what Greenspan wanted to achieve. It's eerie now to think back to a speech, on March 4, 2003, in Orlando, Florida, when he bragged about the fact that consumers had extracted huge amounts of previously built-up equities from owner-occupied homes. For the economy, such equity extraction was financed by *debt.*

The problem has only worsened since 2001. Consumer borrowing has been growing at record annual rates. As of the end of 2004, total consumer debt ended up over $2.1 trillion, a 23 percent increase over four years.[5] When consumer debt reached that amount, it doubled the load shouldered only 10 years before, in 1994, and seemed to set a new record. But in the third quarter of 2007, consumer debt swelled to $2.5 trillion—a 25 percent increase in less than three years. (See Figure 1.1.)

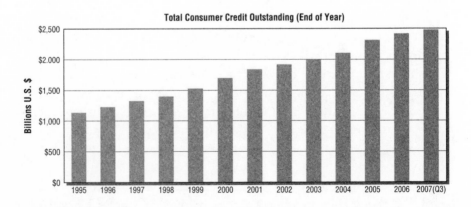

FIGURE 1.1 Consumer Credit Outstanding, 1995–2007
(*Source:* Federal Reserve.)

Annual consumer spending and borrowing continue to rage higher at an annual rate of $480.3 billion. Consumer spending is seen as a positive indicator. That strengthening trend, however, has come from inflating stock and house prices. Debt is soaring, and *that* is the problem. It would be different if that spending was going into a savings and retirement account or, in the case of business, into factory machinery. But it is not. The GDP growth involves spending money *and* borrowing the money rather than using earnings. That's where the problems lie, and that's where the demise of the dollar is going to occur. At some point in the near future, our country is simply going to run out of credit. We're going to max out our monetary credit card.

It is the debt itself, out of control and getting worse, that is going to cause the loss of the dollar's spending power. The higher our consumer debt and our government debt, the weaker the dollar becomes. And that means your savings and retirement account and your Social Security check are going to be worth less and less. This currency crisis is augmented by the fact that China is taking over in the world economy: It is becoming the leading importer, manufacturer, and producer in the world.

TIGHTENING THE BELT

Before the demise of the dollar can be arrested, the causes—runaway debt and U.S. government policy—must be addressed. As a personal investor, there's not much you can do but understand the trends in place and position your portfolio for success. You need to understand *why* prior structural flaws have gotten us to this point. Several things have contributed to this problem, including not only excess credit, but also the lack of savings and investment among American consumers.

A recession is a retreat, a decline in GDP, employment, and trade. Not surprisingly, most people think of such economic forces in terms of lost jobs, which is only one aspect of the bigger picture. But just as recession has an expanded meaning, so does recovery.

In the past, U.S. recessions resulted from tight money and credit. This translates to difficulty in getting loans (especially for homeowners and small businesses). It used to be a symptom of recession that people would say, "Money is tight."

We rarely hear that anymore. Why? Because money isn't ever tight these days; it's just worth less and less. The old-style recession and its accompanying tight money forced consumers and businesses to cut back on borrowing and spending excesses—belt tightening. This change in behavior eventually brought the economy and the financial system back into balance. Cutting back on credit when recession occurs is a form of economic dieting. We have to slim down as a result of tight money, so that the economy can get back into those tight jeans it wore last summer. Most of us know exactly what that is like, and what it means.

Something has changed in the United States. Our economy is fast becoming morbidly obese, and we have long abandoned the desire to slim down. We just keep buying bigger and bigger expectations. We've been living in the bubble.

It became official economic policy under Alan Greenspan's tenure with the Fed not only to accept but to actually *encourage* borrowing and spending excesses. This occurs under the respectable label of "wealth-driven" spending. While he doesn't seem to have the same chronic condition of "interestitis" that afflicted his predecessor, Bernanke has pushed forward four steady rate cuts this year, in August, September, October, and December.

When we speak at conferences and talk to people around the country, we're consistently surprised at how little people actually know about the money they pack away in their wallets. Since 1913 and the passage of the Federal Reserve Act, the federal government has ceded the power over money expressly given to it by the Constitution to private interests. Article I of our Constitution gives *Congress* the power to coin money and to regulate its value. But that power has been delegated to the Fed, which is essentially a banking cartel and *not* part of Congress. This isn't just politics or stuffy economics. By allowing the Fed to have this power, we have no direct voice in how monetary policy is set, not that it would do much good anyway. The loss of sound money—money backed by a tangible asset, rather than a government process—is the root imbalance that's plaguing the dollar.

To give you an idea of how the recession and recovery trend has changed, look at the historical numbers—the *real* numbers and not the political/economic numbers we are being fed. Early in 2007,

President George W. Bush released a budget in which the ledger shifts from red to black and shows a nice surplus, of $61 billion, by 2012. But—and this is a big *but*—it assumes real government spending growth of 0.4 percent a year. Bush has been racking up real growth at the rate of 4.6 percent since he took office in 2001, compared with 2.7 percent under Ronald Reagan and 0.8 percent under Bill Clinton. As the Federal Reserve Bank of Dallas wrote in April 2007, "Washington's fiscal fitness remains a matter of concern. . . . The most recent proposal envisions eliminating them [budget deficits] within six years, but doing so will require lawmakers to overcome several significant obstacles."[6]

And we all know, unfortunately, that's not likely to happen, given the fiscal leadership we've seen so far.

The peak-to-trough changes shown in past recessions make the point: We're not gaining and losing economic weight and returning to previous health in the same way; something has changed drastically and, like a Florida sinkhole, we're slowly going under.

That's why the dollar crisis is invisible. We really don't want to think about it, and the Fed enables us to ignore it by telling us that all is well. As long as credit card companies keep giving us more cards and increasing our credit limits, why worry? And that, in a nutshell, defines the economic problem behind the demise.

An economist would shrug off these changes as cyclical or simply as signs that in the latest recovery a bias toward consumption is affecting outcome. But what does that mean? If, in fact, we are no longer willing to accept tight money as a reality in the down part of the economic cycle, how can we sustain economic growth? How much is going to be enough? And what will happen when seemingly infinite credit and debt excesses finally catch up with us?

CHAPTER 2

FICTITIOUS CAPITALISM AND THE iPOD ECONOMY

> People seem to take it for granted that financial values can be created endlessly out of thin air. Turn the direction and mention that financial values can disappear into nowhere and they insist that it isn't possible.
>
> —Robert Prechter, *Conquer the Crash*

Economists like talking about the gross domestic product (GDP) because it is a big melting pot. But it's misleading. All we have to do is look one by one at the parts that make up GDP and we will see the real trends. The way the news is reported is itself an economic illusion. Our manufacturing base—a historical source of good jobs and economic growth—is undergoing a multidecade trend that is harming our dollar's value. Starting in the late 1970s, the trend involves the loss of manufacturing plants and jobs overseas; and it has gotten worse during the past few years, a hidden indicator.

In past recoveries, industrial production always led the way; it was a dependable sign to measure the strength or weakness of the recovery. Production surged by an average of about 18 percent in the first two years after the typical recession. Since November 2001, though, when the so-called current economic expansion began, industrial production—the creation of goods and the traditional driver of the economy—has barely moved. In fact, the total number of factory jobs lost since the start of the most recent recession in March 2001 is 2.8 million. (We have lost a total of 3.4 million jobs since 1998.) This was the single greatest percentage fall in the labor force in almost eight decades since the Great Depression of the 1930s. What has been happening to American manufacturing can only be described with the word *depression*. And yet this important trend is almost invisible if we look at overall GDP.

This loss in industrial base is not a temporary thing. It is a sharp downward plunge within a longer-term trend—going south and with the dollar's spending power soon to follow unless we turn it around. How does the loss of manufacturing jobs play into the true economic picture and, by association, the dollar crisis? Putting it another way, how is the news spun by the media?

In one headline on the topic in 2003, when the fallout from the 2001 recession was still being felt, we read: "Jobs: The Turning Point Is Here."[1] What was even more interesting in that story was a table titled "A Jobless Recovery? That Depends." Obviously, the author wanted to convey the message that the dismal employment picture was offset by good news elsewhere in the economy. But in fact, the story's statistics only confirmed that the U.S. economy is in a wrenching crisis. Today a more timely news headline is "Making Less Than Dad," published on May 25, 2007, on CNN. The production side with high-paying jobs is disappearing, while the consumption side with low-paying jobs is booming. Check the numbers.

As shown in Figure 2.1, since the end of 2001, the main job losses have occurred in the following sectors (in thousands):

Manufacturing	2,264
Telecommunication services	329
Air transportation	128
Computer systems design and related services	20

Losses in manufacturing have almost doubled, while computer systems design and services have dropped nearly 80 percent.

And here is where employment has grown (also in thousands):

Health care and social assistance	1,786
Accommodation and food service	1,005
Government	872
Construction	863
Temporary help services	293
Real estate	163
Wholesale trade	125
Commercial banking	61

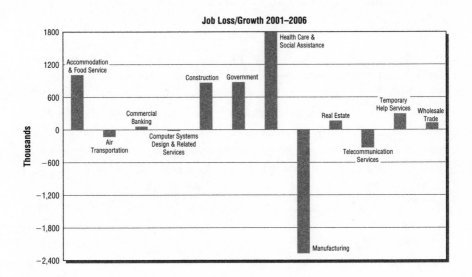

FIGURE 2.1   Job Loss and Growth, 2001–2006
(*Source:* Bureau of Labor Statistics.)

The gains in construction, commercial banking, and real estate were directly related to the housing and mortgage refinancing bubble, and now, with the growing number of foreclosures that are mounting as the fallout continues into 2008, in two of these sectors growth comes from refinancing and not from any form of productive activity.

Look at the phenomenal growth in accommodation and services— 10 times the numbers just a few years ago—and at temporary help services, which more than doubled. What does such growth say about our real productivity? This employment record shows just how the economy's grossly distorted spending and growth pattern is moving. While the production side is collapsing, the consumption side is expanding.

Our economy is changing in big, big ways. We are moving away from goods production and toward services. It is a development that American policy makers and economists have hailed as a normal and natural shift in emphasis for a developed economy. This complacent view ignores two important points, though. First, the manufacturing sector pays the highest wages, which makes it a no-brainer for anyone to understand—especially anyone who has lost a manufacturing job and who now works in the retail sector. Second, manufacturing is the source of earnings that pay for the overseas obligations of every country. After a slight dip in 2005 to 53 percent, the United States is now at the point where our exports are at only 56 percent of our imports (57 percent, if you count the gold shipped out of the country). We know that manufacturing produces more and more goods while employing fewer and fewer people. But the American case is different; the production of goods increasingly lags behind growth in personal income. But so what? How does the balance of trade affect the typical American, and how does it hurt the dollar?

We read in our media that miraculous productivity gains have become the main driver of U.S. GDP growth. But is this for real, or is it only a big economic hoax? We may hear a variety of possible explanations. For example, businesses are supposed to be able to squeeze more value out of the average worker. As this idea boosts profits, the impending comeback of business investment spending is taken for granted. The concept of improved productivity is supposed to offset lost market share in a global sense.

Labor productivity is an economic indicator that tells us how efficiently people work. In 2004—the year we supposedly put the recession behind us—labor productivity in business, which covers 70 percent of all labor productivity—sank to 2.9 percent. And in 2005 and 2006, the drop was really alarming: 2 percent and 1 percent, respectively. That will explain why the government jumped up and down about the surge in the third quarter of 2007. But keep in mind what I said earlier about surges. They imply that things are improving. This would be true if, at the same time, average wages were growing or at least keeping pace. The claim is contradicted by the numbers. The United States is going through an employment shift away from high-paying manufacturing jobs into low-paying jobs, in sectors like health services and retail.

If you want to make the hair on your head stand on end, check out the numbers from a recent survey by the Center on Budget and Policy Priorities, which studied data from the Commerce Department going back to 1929. In 2006, the share of national income that went to wages and salaries was the lowest on record. Since the 2001 recession, wages and salaries grew on average 1.9 percent annually, compared with corporate profits at 12.8 percent. In previous recoveries, wages and salaries grew at an average annual rate of 3.8 percent—that's nearly twice the recent rate—while corporate profits grew at 8.3 percent, about two-thirds the recent rate.

The belief that productivity growth is the whole deal is delusional, but as an economic principle it is unique to American economists. In contrast, European economists rarely mentioned the notion. They know about the importance of productivity growth, but they view it as part of a more important trend, capital investment. American economists don't like to go there, because it brings up the real problem with the relationship between employment and the value of the dollar. As a rule, where there is high capital investment, high productivity growth can also be taken for granted. And by the way, capital investment also provides the increase in demand and spending necessary to translate growing productivity into effectively higher employment and economic growth.

This concept—another no-brainer—is known to anyone who has studied history. The creation of jobs is part of the creation of infrastructure. In the United States of the nineteenth century, an era of building great railroads and canals created unprecedented economic growth and jobs. Those jobs were not created in the vacuum of a passive economy.

So here we find ourselves, in the enigma of high productivity growth along with plunging employment. Why? Well, the American economists have the explanation, as always: High productivity growth goes hand in hand with jobless economic growth.

It's possible. But it might be worth pointing out that it has never happened before. It's a little like saying we can expect workers to work harder if we give them pay cuts. Higher productivity has always accompanied job creation, and that comes directly from capital investment. Old-fashioned productivity growth also involves genuine wealth creation through the building of factories and installation of machinery. The country's most recent productivity growth had nothing to do with capital investment, sadly. Net investment has collapsed.

There is only one logical explanation for this contrary indicator: It must have more statistical than economic causes. Are we to believe in numbers or in economics? If we select economics, then we have to confront the facts: There is no reasonable economic explanation for the reported trend. The doubtful accuracy in reported productivity begins with the fact that real GDP growth is vastly overstated. This is due to inflation rates that have been systematically trimmed to the downside—falsified, if you will, to present a conclusion that is just not realistic. GDP is supposed to mean *growth* in the domestic economy. In practice, the numbers are not only inaccurate; they are misleading.

Around the world, inflation is based on measuring price changes. In the United States, we have moved away from that idea. Our economists prefer measuring consumer satisfaction or confidence. As a result, quality improvements and the so-called substitution effect play a key role in reducing reported inflation. *Substitution* refers to the way consumers alter their pattern of purchases as prices change. If beef prices rise, the consumer buys chicken. If air travel is too expensive, people drive or take a train or bus.

Our economic reporting system is like a vast national used car dealership, complete with fashion-challenged salespeople. We are being sold a lemon. The statistical gimmick of how inflation is reported, for example, means that our actual inflation rates are understated by around two percentage points per year, based on how the same trend is measured in other countries. The result: overstatement of GDP.

So inflation is higher than we think, and the GDP is not growing as well as we have been told. In assessing the value of our dollars on an after-tax and after-inflation basis, we are losing spending power. If we use the phony government inflation number, we are not even breaking even. This problem is not limited to how our savings and investment values are being eroded. It goes far beyond the cost of milk or tomatoes.

If we look at changes in business investment, what do we find?

According to conventional reports, a great rebound in business investment spending is already in full swing, primarily in the high-tech sector. But the so-called investment rebound comes completely from the way we price computers. You'd have to have a Ph.D. in "statistical economics" to understand the method used by the Bureau of Economic Analysis (BEA) to account for price declines in the computer industry brought on by natural competition for their products.

"The inflation-adjusted figure for investment in computers is no longer published," is the way the BEA describes it, "because [the U.S. Department of] Commerce was concerned the rapid price declines for computers made the figures misleading."

Doesn't that statement seem odd? The reported rate of productivity growth comes from the potential production of computers, not from their actual use. But all the talk of the high productivity effects of computers logically relates to such effects from their use, of which we know nothing. Why? *Because they are impossible to measure.* The pricing of computers creates absurdly exaggerated perceptions of the money being spent and earned on computers—resulting in correspondingly higher GDP growth.

For example, under such a pricing scheme, computer producers reported an increase in revenue of $128.2 billion, or 49 percent, from $262.1 billion to $390.3 billion between first quarter 2002 and third quarter 2003. Very nice. *But* in actual dollars, the gain was only $16.4 billion, from $71.9 billion to $88.3 billion. BEA's inflated report created a boom for what was, in effect, a trickle. From an economic perspective, this contrast is huge, and the phony numbers are what most people use to draw conclusions.

Given the disparities between economic reporting and the real world, the economic importance of high-tech industries has been and continues to be overhyped in the United States. In terms of sales, employment, and earned profits, it is a sector of minor importance. The high-tech profit performance has been abysmal. Remember the industrial revolution and its lessons. Implementing new technologies involves radical changes across the economies, requiring and creating huge new industries with soaring employment. It radically changes economic and personal life. Is our so-called technological revolution a new industrial revolution? Hardly. By comparison, the new high-tech industries—what Andy Kessler refers to as the iPod Economy—are marginal. At the very least, measuring production based on these sectors is deceptive.

PROFIT RENAISSANCE—OR PROFITABILITY HOAX?

Under the official methodology—meaning reports from the government and from the official National Income and Product Accounts (NIPA)[2]—the profit picture is impressive. But a variety of profit studies tell a different story. Most economists have a great liking for the most comprehensive figure: corporate profits with inventory valuation and capital consumption adjustments. This is a fuzzy number. For one thing, it obscures what is really going on in the trend, as it includes the financial sector and now exceeds $1.6 trillion. Since their lows during the recessionary years, the aggregate numbers have grown by about 60 percent. But including the financial sector is a problem.

In what we may term the "real economy" (i.e., excluding the financial sector) the numbers are quite different. This nonfinancial real economy experienced pretax profits at a low of $357.2 billion in 2001 from a peak of $573.4 billion in 1997. Even with gradually increasing reported profits through 2006 (reaching $814.3 billion by the third quarter) the numbers remain, well, flat. This is true when we look at manufacturing alone, where we find that the numbers are no higher than they were in the previous decade. The gain for the nonfinancial sector has overwhelmingly come from retail trade, and we have to confront what this means in terms of jobs as well as profits. When we compare typical manufacturing profits and see a decade-long flat line, it is difficult to justify claims of an improved economy.

This economic aberration in our reported GDP numbers—what our leaders have generously called growth—has not occurred simply because home-owning consumers replaced their income losses by heavy borrowing against rising house prices. While income-driven spending slumped, bubble-driven spending surged, and that implicitly gave a big boost to profits. Income-driven spending derives from wages and salaries, which—from another point of view—are also business expenses. In contrast, credit-financed spending increases business revenues.

Now we apply the same logic to what happens in the economy as a whole. Just as a corporation is limited in how far it can improve its bottom line, the consumer is also subject to economic laws. What turned cost cutting of the past few years into profits for businesses was a debt-driven economy. Consumers increased their spending despite heavy losses, and funded it through higher borrowing. We see the economic flaw in this more than anywhere else in the U.S. trade deficit.

CHAPTER 3

PATHOLOGICAL CONSUMPTION

I've spent a lot of money on booze, birds, and fast cars—the rest
I just squandered.

—George Best

Most people can relate to the realities of how jobs and profits shift,
and why. The idea that higher-wage manufacturing jobs are being
lost and replaced by lower-wage retail jobs, for example, is a reality
that working people understand. They get it. The same is not always
true when we talk about trade deficits. Like the falling dollar itself,
it's worth asking the question: How does it affect you, the individual?

The trade deficit—the excess of imports over exports—has a direct
and serious effect on the value of our dollars. As long as we continue
having big trade deficits, it means we're spending more money overseas than we're making at home. Our manufacturing profits are lower
than our consumption. If your family's budget has a "trade deficit" of
sorts, you'll soon be in trouble. If your spouse spends $4,000 for every
$2,000 you bring home, something eventually gives way. This is what
is going on with the trade deficit.

In fact, the trade deficit is one of the most important trends in the
economy, and the one most likely to affect the value of the dollar.

Combined with our government's big budget deficit, the trade
deficit only accelerates the speed of decline in our dollar's value.

Speaking in terms of spending power of the dollar, the trade deficit is the third rail of the economy. Here is what has been going on: The United States used to produce goods and sell them not only here at home, but throughout the world. We led the way, but not anymore. The shift away from dominance in the production of things people need has allowed other countries (most notably China and India, and with Colombia, Russia, Brazil, and Mexico not far behind) to pass us up, and now the U.S. consumer has become a *buyer* instead of a *seller.* This international version of conspicuous consumption[1] is financed not from the profits of commerce, but from debt. Let's think about this for a minute. If we were buying from domestic profits, the trade deficit wouldn't be such a bad thing. It would mean we were spending money earned from domestic productivity. But this is *not* what is going on. We are going further and further *into debt* to buy goods from other countries. Our wealth is being transferred overseas and, at the same time, we are sinking deeper into debt. This is taking place individually as well as nationally. Consumer debt (you know: credit cards, mortgages, lines of credit) is growing to record levels, and the federal current account deficit is moving our multitrillion-dollar national debt into new high territory.

Sure, we should be concerned about retirement income from savings, investments, pension plans, and Social Security. But a bigger danger is that, even with a comfortable retirement nest egg by today's standards, what if those dollars are worthless when we retire? What then?

The big question today is, how long can this debt-driven economy continue? If you quit your job and refinance your home, you could live for a while on the money. The higher your equity, the longer you would be able to spend, spend, spend. But then what?

This is precisely what is going on in the U.S. economy, and, at some point very soon, we are going to have to face up to it and change our ways. The trade deficit is the best way to track what's going on. Returning to the analogy of quitting your job and living off of your home equity, you may stay home all day and order an endless array of electronics, furniture, toys, computers, and the like; in other words, you could consume goods in place of working. But remember, you didn't win the lottery; you are financing this new plan with borrowed money. The lender will want that repaid. So this individual version of a trade deficit (the deficit between generating income and spending money) is what is happening on a national level in the United States.

This is the problem that is directly affecting the value of the dollar; and the situation is getting worse. We know that the dollar is in trouble because we see it depreciating against the floating currencies of other countries.

The United States has a lot of wealth, but that wealth is being consumed very quickly. History shows that no matter how rich you are, you can lose that wealth if you're not productive. Meanwhile, the dollar's value falls and—in spite of the Fed's view that this is a good thing—it means our savings are worth less. Your spending power falls when the dollar falls, and as this continues, the consequences will be sobering.

The dollar's plunge has taken many people, currency experts of banks included, by surprise. For many of them, it is still impossible to grasp. Some talking head on CNBC said that he was at a complete loss to understand how such weak economies as those seen in the European Union could have a strong currency. For American policy makers and most economists, the huge trade deficit is no problem. They find it natural that fast-growing countries import money while slow-growing economies export money. At least, that is the recurring theme.

So Americans traveling abroad may continue to complain that "it has become so expensive to travel in Europe" as though the problem were somehow the fault of the Europeans. But in fact, it is the declining spending power of the dollar that is to blame, and not just the French, the Italians, and the residents of the so-called chocolate-making countries.

This problem is pegged not to some speculative or fuzzy economic cause, even though the concept of currency exchange rates continues to mystify. A historically large trade deficit is at the core of the declining dollar. Somebody needs to get over the notion that our economy is strong and other economies are weak, merely because this is America. In the United States, the reason for the trade deficit is not a high rate of investment as we see in some other countries, but an abysmally low level of national savings. We are spending, not producing.

A second argument offered by some is that "capital flows from high-saving countries to low-saving countries, wanting to grow faster." Under this reasoning, a deficit country, looking at both consumption and investment, is absorbing more than its own production. But whether this is good or bad for the economy depends on the source and use of foreign funds. Do those funds pay for the financing of consumption in excess of production (as in the United States) or for investment in excess of saving? That is the key question that ought to be asked in the first place about the huge U.S. capital imports.

To quote Joan Robinson, a well-known economist in the 1920s and 1930s close to John Maynard Keynes:

> If the capital inflows merely permit an excess of consumption over production, the economy is on the road to ruin. If they permit an excess of investment over home saving, the result depends on the nature of the investment.[2]

The huge U.S. capital inflows (economic jargon for money coming into the country), accounting now for more than 6 percent of gross domestic product (GDP), have not financed productive investment; in fact, they are financing more and more debt. Capital grew from 5 percent in 2005 to more than 6 percent in 2006, according to a report from the Bureau of Economic Analysis (BEA), "U.S. International Investment Position." Our net investments are among the lowest in the world, meaning we prefer spending and borrowing over actual production and growth. The huge capital inflows have not helped finance a higher rate of investment. The United States has been selling its factories and financial assets to pay for consumption.

It's helpful to use a *real* means for measuring economic strength. Money coming here from overseas finances higher personal consumption. The steep decline in personal saving is a symptom of our spending, and along with that habit we have lower capital investment and a growing federal budget deficit. In the third quarter of 2005, for the first time ever, the rate actually fell into negative territory—to −1 percent.

The U.S. economy has for years been the strongest in the world, leading the rest of the countries. Our *Daily Reckoning* newsletter routinely gets reader responses saying, in effect, "How dare you impugn the superiority of the American economy! How dare you!" We're rather thick-skinned, so the insults bounce off rather easily. But "facts are stubborn things."[3] The fact that the U.S. economy has outperformed the rest of the world in the past several years is easily explained: Our credit machine has been operating in overdrive nonstop. It is geared to accommodate unlimited credit for two purposes—consumption and financial speculation. Let's look at these two things a little more deeply.

Credit is not the same thing as production, despite the fuzzy logic you get from the financial media. There is a severe imbalance between the huge amount of credit that goes into the economy and the minimal amount that goes into productive investment. Instead of moving to rein in these excesses and imbalances, under Greenspan, the Fed clearly opted to sustain and even to encourage them. I want to believe that under Bernanke, the Fed will do better, but so far, it is still customary to measure economic strength by simply comparing recent real GDP growth rates. It is pointed to as proof and applauded by U.S. economists when U.S. economic growth outscores Europe—like some kind of dysfunctional *futbol* match.

Financial speculation is equally unproductive. An investor puts up capital to generate a sustained and long-term growth plan. For example, buying and holding stocks is a form of investment and a sign that the investor has faith in the management of that company.

Speculators don't care about long-term growth. They want to get in and out of positions as quickly as possible, make a profit, and repeat the process. So speculative profits—especially those paid for with borrowed money—tend to be churned over and over in further speculation *and* increased spending. None of that money goes into investment in the long-term sense. The speculator is invested in short-term profits, nothing more. Even so, the speculator is today's cowboy, the risk-taking, living-on-the-edge market hero willing to take big chances. He is seen as a guy with big stones because he's staring the prospect of loss right in the eye.

A PENNY BORROWED IS A PENNY EARNED

The U.S. economy is based on the belief that in practice, borrowing is a type of wealth generation. The trouble is . . . it's not. Economic policy and growth are going to reflect how consumers spend what they have, individually and as a nation. The critical question to ask is: How much of our overall current production is devoted to consumption and how much to capital investment? In defining economic health and strength, generations of economists have focused on two economic indicators: savings and investment. It used to be a truism among economists of all schools of thought that the growth of an economy's tangible capital stock was the key determinant of increased productivity and subsequently of good, high-paying jobs. And it also used to be a truism that tangible capital investment in factories, production equipment, and commercial and residential building represents the one and only form of genuine wealth creation.

Not so anymore. The United States has abandoned these beliefs, even though they are obvious and, well, true. The laws of economics haven't been revoked, but the wonks in Washington behave as if they have.

THE AMERICAN MONEY CULTURE

To Americans, the suggestion that the dollar is losing value is unthinkable—unpatriotic even. The problem is found not only in the lack of understanding about the nature of wealth and the investments used to create and sustain it; in our money culture, policy makers and economists make no distinction between wealth created through saving and investment in the real economy versus "wealth" created in the markets through asset bubbles brought about by credit policies. Even when suggestions about the flaw in this thinking arise, the distraction of consumerism has created a type of attention deficit disorder. We're trying to tell people to lose weight while meeting with them for lunch at the soda fountain.

We not only spend at a high level; we also prefer accumulating wealth on the same fast track. Traditionally, economists recognized that it took time to build an estate. People and countries could build wealth slowly. But today

> the new approach requires that a state find ways to increase the market value of its productive assets. [In such a strategy] an economic policy that aims to achieve growth by wealth creation therefore does not attempt to increase the production of goods and services, except as a secondary objective.[4]

This a perfect description of the economic thinking that rules in the United States today, not only in corporations and the financial markets, but even among policy makers, elevating wealth creation—that is, bubble creation—to the ultimate in economic wisdom. The asset bubbles in recent years—in stocks, bonds, and housing—were primary elements of economic growth. Considering, though, the lopsided effect on consumer spending and borrowing, is this a reasonable and sustainable policy? Should it be encouraged? It works in the short run from the demand side, but where does it lead? Just as mercantilism in eighteenth-century Europe ultimately fell under its own weight, the modern economic trend toward house-of-cards wealth creation may become a twenty-first-century version of past lessons not fully learned or appreciated.

America's grinding credit machine makes all the difference in economic growth and wealth creation between our country and the rest of the world. Lately, China is overtaking the United States in so many ways, but, ironically, based on a more tangible economic viewpoint. It may prove to be the great irony of the twenty-first century that the Chinese—once viewed as the most puristic of the Communist regimes, rabidly anticapitalist at the height of their fervor—may turn out to be the *most successful* model of worldwide capitalism. (On a recent trip to China, I had a good chuckle while touring the Forbidden Palace in Beijing. The tour was sponsored by Nestlé, and the plaques that explained where the concubines slept had American Express logos in the lower-right corners.)

China's growth is no laughing matter. It is investment-driven, with a capital investment rate close to 43 percent of GDP in 2006. GDP growth increased to 10.7 percent that year, and then rose by 11.1 percent in the first quarter of 2007. But the country's investment rate isn't the only record—in 2005, personal saving reached 52 percent of GDP, according to an envious U.S. Treasury. By U.S. standards, that is very, very high.

SERIAL BUBBLE BLOWERS

According to the consensus view, the U.S. economy is breaking out of its anemic growth pattern. A few signs of accelerating economic improvement are gleefully cited to support this forecast: the

3.9 percent spurt of "real GDP growth" in the third quarter of 2007; higher investment technology spending, up 9 percent in 2006; surging profits; and surging early indicators, among them, in particular, indicators such as the Institute for Supply Management (ISM) survey for manufacturing.[5]

We hear that various indicators are at their strongest in 20 years. But do we simply accept the popular wisdom? No, because many of the reported indicators are nonrecurring. If they aren't really signs of a sustained pattern, the results are dubious at best. For example, the impressive third quarter 2003 growth spurt was the direct result of a one-time splurge in federal tax rebates and a flurry of mortgage refinancing caused by low interest rates. In the third quarter of 2007, we had similarly impressive results, GDP growth of 3.9 percent. But you've got to read between the lines: Growth was fueled by personal consumption, which doubled to over 3 percent, and export growth in goods, the largest bump up since the fourth quarter of 1996. Housing values fell, foreclosures accelerated, and imports grew, a by now familiar economic refrain in 2007.

As to investment spending, what is really going on? So-called investment in housing is now distorted by the escalating foreclosures and credit crisis caused by the subprime mortgage mess. What should matter is the change in total nonresidential investment—business factories and equipment, for example—a trend that has been flat for many years. There is no real growth in business investment. In 2006, growth increased by a mere 2.7 percent—half of 2005's 5.6 percent and considerably short of 2004's 9.7 percent. Looked at as a percentage of GDP, that's only a puny 2.1 percent.

The U.S. economy's so-called improvement has one main reason: All the economic growth of the "recovery" years since 2001 can be traced to a seemingly endless array of asset and borrowing bubbles. Quoting analyst Stephen Roach, "The Fed, in effect, has become a serial bubble blower"—first the stock market bubble; then the bond bubble; then the housing bubble and the mortgage refinancing bubble. As a result, consumer spending has been surging well in excess of disposable income for years. But we must understand, this is not *real* growth.

The idea behind the bubble economy was that sustained and rising consumer spending would eventually stimulate investment spending. This is like suggesting that overeating will eventually lead to serious dieting. As you might expect, rising consumer spending has not had the desired effect. In fact, consumer spending will slow down when consumer borrowing starts to fade. And that's just a matter of time.

The dollar is going to continue falling over the long run. It will fall as long as we continue to outspend our investment and production rates. If foreign investors were to slash their investment levels in the U.S. dollar and Treasury securities, that would cause a hard landing. Our credit would dry up rapidly. This would not just send the dollar crashing. A sudden rupture of private capital would also hammer the U.S. bond and stock markets.

Private foreign investment into U.S. assets has slumped. But we are addicted to foreign investment; this is where much of our consumer credit and debt is financed. So we are vulnerable if our credit economy is supported primarily by huge holdings of dollars on the part of foreign private and institutional investors. If the dollar's fall begins to frighten foreign owners, they will sell from this immense stock of dollar assets.

How big are these foreign holdings? We rarely hear about this problem on the financial news channels, so what's the big deal? Well, let's run the numbers. At the end of 2006, foreign holdings of U.S. dollars had a market value of $16.295 trillion. This includes corporate and government bonds held directly and by foreign governments. It's a big number. The point here is that these huge foreign dollar holdings are a looming threat to the dollar, perhaps the biggest threat of all. If these foreign investors lose confidence in the U.S. economy and the dollar, they will sell and switch the dollar proceeds into a stronger currency.

That $16.295 trillion is a lot of debt. A lot. How is it going to get repaid? And by whom?

The hope in Washington is that the declining value of the dollar will reduce the U.S. trade deficit. Past experience shows that this is unlikely. The chronic U.S. trade deficit is caused by exceptionally high levels of consumption, undersaving, and underinvestment. Improving the trade deficit would require a major correction of these imbalances, and cannot be fixed simply by watching the dollar's value continue to decline.

An economic downturn would come as a rude awakening to most Americans, a cataclysmic shock. It would directly affect the other two asset bubbles, housing and stocks, in addition to the dollar value bubble itself. Imagine the uncertainty and turmoil this will create in the financial markets. Rock solid? We think not.

The U.S. economy is much weaker and much more vulnerable than official statistics make it seem. The Fed cushioned the impact of the bursting stock market bubble by manipulating new asset bubbles. Ultralow short-term interest rates and the promise to keep them there for a long time have fueled a housing and mortgage borrowing boom, which also extended the consumer borrowing-and-spending binge. "Happy days are here again." Indeed.

While European policy makers and economists worry endlessly about budget deficits and slow growth, their counterparts on this side of the pond continue to boast how wonderfully efficient and flexible the U.S. economy is. Negative national savings, a growing trade deficit, never-ending budget deficits, the subprime mortgage mess, and the credit crisis—all these and any other imbalances and dislocations are nonproblems. The official word is that the exploding credit and ballooning debt in the United States are not signs of excess, but a testament to the financial system's extraordinary efficiency.

Small prediction: A shock awaits the "nonproblem" crowd when we finally confront our economic realities. The U.S. inflation rate is understated by at least 1.5 percentage points per year through the economic/statistical magic of grossly overstating real GDP and productivity growth. Bond king Bill Gross discovered this fact of life and commented on it in 2004.[6] An active proponent of inflation manipulation was former Fed chairman Alan Greenspan, apparently because—and here again we find a recurring theme—"a low inflation rate fosters low interest rates."

The huge credit and debt bubbles in the United States have created a dislocated and imbalanced economy, so that a sustained recovery is going to be impossible without many painful changes. We suffer from a false sense of optimism, and when the implicit promise of that optimism is not met, experts will no longer be able to argue away the dollar's weakness.

Under a system of truly free currency markets, the dollar would have collapsed long ago. But the massive dollar purchases by the Asian central banks have prevented this. China's persistence in pegging its currency to the dollar traps other Asian countries into doing the same.

This practice creates a credit bubble that, in turn, distorts economic growth. In contrast, the European Central Bank is firmly opposed to currency intervention. In its view, artificial tinkering in the currency markets tends to fuel credit excess. It could be right, using the U.S. economy as an example.

Those who like currency intervention policy—artificially controlling the value of the dollar, in essence—ignore the beneficial effects of a rising currency. The benefit is twofold. First, it reduces the trade deficit and makes us more competitive with our trade partners. Second, it also adds a healthy premium to domestic purchasing power. It's important, though, to make a distinction here. Under our present system, our purchasing power is based exclusively on borrowed money. Under a system of competitive trade and a higher dollar, our purchasing power would be based on real economic forces, and not on good credit alone.

The lengthy pegging of Asian currencies to the U.S. dollar will eventually lead to an economic crisis in both the United States and Asia, because the central banks accommodate each other's credit and spending excesses. So we have to change the system so that competitive forces can work and replace currency intervention as international policy.

A weakened U.S. economy shouldn't surprise anyone. It is a direct result of the questionable nature of the so-called economic recovery. The U.S. economy is plagued by an array of growth-inhibiting imbalances: the trade deficit, the federal budget deficit, household indebtedness, a negative personal saving rate, and, of course, record-high consumer spending. Any other country faced with these imbalances would have collapsed long ago. But the U.S. dollar was spared this fate when Asian central banks began accumulating the dollars needed to avoid rises in their currencies.

Both the United States and China practice credit excess, but with a crucial difference: In the United States, the credit excesses went into higher asset prices and, more notably, into personal consumption. In Asia, credit excesses went into capital investment and production. The result is an odd disparity between the two economies: Americans borrow and consume, and the Asians produce.

This symbiosis plays out in the trade gap. Ironically, this ever-growing problem is ignored on the national level and plays virtually no role in U.S. economic policy or analysis. Since 1999, the trade deficit as a share of GDP has nearly tripled, from 2.1 percent to 5.75 percent. In comparison, during the 1980s, policy makers and economists worried about the harm that trade deficits were causing in U.S. manufacturing. In a September 1985 move orchestrated by James Baker, the U.S. Treasury secretary, the finance ministers of the G-5 nations[7] agreed to drive the dollar sharply down in concerted action.

By the mid-1990s U.S. policy makers had decided that trade deficits were beneficial for the U.S. economy and its financial markets. Cheap imports were playing an important role in preventing inflation and, as a result, higher interest rates. Had the decision been to allow interest rates to rise, it would have had the effect of slowing down consumer spending. Instead, spending is out of control and the trade gap is the consequence. Ultimately, the victim in all of this is going to be the U.S. dollar.

The economic cycle involving inflation, higher interest rates, monetary tightening, recession, and recovery has a predictable postwar pattern in the United States and in the rest of the world. But we've taken a departure from this for the first time. A critic might argue that now the United States is enjoying a prolonged period of strong economic growth with low inflation and low interest rates. What could be bad about that?

Well, what's bad about that is the fact that we are *not* experiencing strong economic growth. U.S. net business investment has fallen to all-time postwar lows, little more than 2 percent of GDP in recent years. At the same time, net financial investment is running at about 7.8 percent of GDP. In other words, the counterpart to foreign investment in the U.S. economy has been higher private and public consumption, accompanied by lower saving and investment.

Official opinion in America says that the huge U.S. trade gap is mainly the fault of foreigners, for two reasons. One is the eagerness of foreign investors to acquire U.S. assets with higher returns than in the rest of the world; the other is supposed to be weaker economic growth in the rest of the world. In this view, the trade gap directly results from foreign investment because it provides the dollars that the foreign investors need.

FROM KNOW-HOW TO NOWHERE

The first thing to realize about a deficit in foreign trade is that, by definition, it reflects an excess of domestic spending over domestic output. But such spending excess is actually caused by overly liberal credit at home, and not really by cheaper goods produced elsewhere.

Just as shaky is the second argument, ascribing the trade gap to higher U.S. economic growth. Asian countries, in particular China, have much higher rates of economic growth than the United States. Yet they all run a chronic trade surplus, which is caused by high savings rates. This is the crucial variable concerning trade surplus or trade deficit.

The diversion of U.S. domestic spending to foreign producers is, in effect, a loss of revenue for businesses and consumers in the United States. Is this important? Yes. The loss is a heart-stopping $759 billion in 2006, up more than 50 percent from a $500 billion deficit just a few years earlier. This is America's income and profit killer, and it can't be fixed with *more* credit and *more* consumption. This serious drag of the growing trade gap on U.S. domestic incomes and profits would have bred slower economic growth, if not recession, long ago. This has so far been delayed by the Fed's extreme monetary looseness, creating artificial domestic demand growth through credit expansion.

The need for ever-greater credit and debt creation just to offset the income losses caused by the trade gap is one of our big problems. An equally big problem is a distortion of the numbers. We are officially in great shape, but the numbers don't support this belief. Personal consumption in the past few years has increased real GDP at the expense of savings, while business investment has grown only moderately.

This can only end badly. Normally, tight money forces consumers and businesses to unwind their excesses during recessions. But in the latest round, the Fed's loose monetary stance has *stepped up* consumers' spending excesses. Our weight trainer is feeding us Big Macs. If we were to measure economic health by credit expansion, the United States has the worst inflation in history. And still our experts are puzzled by a soaring import surplus.

The problem here is that American policy makers and economists fail to understand the significance of the damage that is being caused by monetary excess and the growing trade gap. The trade gap is hailed as a sign of superior economic growth, while the hyperinflation in stock and house prices is hailed as wealth creation.

Until the late 1960s, total international reserves of central banks hovered below $100 billion. At the end of 2003, they exceeded $3 trillion, of which two-thirds was held in dollars. And starting in 2001, the rapid buildup exploded. Foreign reserves now are estimated at $5.6 trillion—but reserves don't include sovereign wealth funds (SWFs), government-owned or -controlled funds, which add another $1.5 trillion to $2.7 trillion. A steep jump in these reserves, an increase of $907 billion, occurred in the years 2000–2002, when Asian central banks, with China and Japan as the main buyers, bought virtually the whole amount. And despite global ups and downs, these two countries are still buying.

And who said economists don't have a sense of humor? In early 2006, before leaving the White House Council of Economic Advisers and joining the Fed as its new chairman, Ben Bernanke suggested that the growing U.S. trade deficit—a bubble the size of 6 percent of our GDP—was not really a deficit but a "savings glut," caused by excessive saving in Asia and Europe. So we can conveniently blame our growing U.S. trade deficit on the rest of the world, which saves too much. It's *their* fault for selling us stuff and then putting all the cash they earn back in the U.S. of A.

It was widely assumed that rising stock and house prices would keep American consumers both willing and able to spend, spend, spend their way to wealth—indefinitely. But that assumption radically changed in 2007, when the housing bubble finally burst.

Also alarming is the transfer of U.S. net worth to interests overseas, which endangers U.S. economic and political health. Case in point: Warren Buffett, who kept his vast fortune invested at home for more than 70 years, decided in 2002 to invest in foreign currencies for the first time. Buffett and the management of Berkshire Hathaway believe the dollar is going to continue its decline. We should not need confirmation such as this to recognize the inevitable; but it bolsters the argument that the dollar is, in fact, in serious trouble, and that this trouble is likely to continue. In addition to debt problems at home,

Buffett made his decision based at least partially on the ever-growing trade deficit. In his most recent letter to Berkshire Hathaway shareholders, Buffett warned:

> As our U.S. trade problems worsen, the probability that the dollar will weaken over time continues to be high. I fervently believe in real trade—the more the better for both us and the world. We had about $1.44 trillion of this honest-to-God trade in 2006. But the U.S. also had $.76 trillion of *pseudo*-trade last year—imports for which we exchanged no goods or services. . . .
>
> Making these purchases that weren't reciprocated by sales, the U.S. necessarily transferred ownership of its assets or IOUs to the rest of the world. Like a very wealthy but self-indulgent family, we peeled off a bit of what we owned in order to consume more than we produced.[8]

Buffett is especially concerned about the transfer of wealth to outside interests. He notes:

> These transfers will have consequences, however. Already the prediction I made last year about one fall-out from our spending binge has come true: The "investment income" account of our country—positive in every previous year since 1915—turned negative in 2006. Foreigners now earn more on their U.S. investments than we do on our investments abroad. In effect, we've used up our bank account and turned to our credit care. And, like everyone who gets in hock, the U.S. will now experience "reverse compounding" as we pay ever-increasing amounts of interest on interest.[9]

CHAPTER 4

SHORT UNHAPPY EPISODES IN MONETARY HISTORY

History is a vast early warning system.

—Norman Cousins

The whole basis for money itself—currency as a means of commerce—is based on tangible value. In other words, money is not the greenbacks we carry around, it is supposed to be the gold or other metal backing it up. The dollar is a promissory note. Check what it says at the top of the bill itself: "Federal Reserve Note."

Today, the American dollars in circulation are just a bunch of IOUs. That would be fine if the gold reserves were sitting in Fort Knox to back up those IOUs . . . but they are not. The Fed just keeps printing more and more money and it will eventually catch up with us. The day will come when we will have to pay off those IOUs, not only domestically but to the ever-expanding foreign investors, too.

We can look at gold in a couple of ways: as the basis for solid asset value, or as a tangible investment with its own supply and demand market. Many people today shy away from gold because of the incredible price movement between 1971 and 1980. This occurred following two important and critical events. In 1971, President Nixon took the United States system off the gold standard (meaning we could print as much money as we want, right?). And then in 1974, President Gerald Ford removed a 40-year-old restriction on Americans' right to own gold.

Looking back to 1933, the Great Depression caused a serious gold shortage. The Emergency Banking Relief Act of 1933 was passed "to provide relief in the existing national emergency in banking and for other purposes. . . ."[1]

The bill required all citizens to turn over gold coin and currency in exchange for Federal Reserve notes. Refusing to turn over gold carried a $10,000 fine and 10 years in jail. This unusual move was intended to prevent the public from hoarding gold bullion. The solution was a simple one: make it illegal to own gold directly. But as is often the case when a government acts under emergency powers, this critical law started the ball rolling toward the trouble our dollar is in today.

Once Nixon removed currency from the gold standard and Ford removed the restriction on owning gold, the price shot up from the regulated $35 per ounce. It topped out above $800 by January 1980 and then fell rapidly back to $253 by 1999, its low point. But we should not look at this price gyration as any market-driven force behind gold as an investment. The climb and subsequent fall were caused by government intervention over a 40-year period. We have to look at the price movement as an overreaction to the whole gold-to-currency relationship.

On January 31, 2008, gold hit $936 per ounce, climbing once more, not in overreaction mode but, finally, in market mode. Take a look at gold as a strong defensive investment given the current economic situation and trend. Here are four compelling arguments:

1. *The trade gap.* The U.S. trade surplus of years ago has disappeared. Is it a coincidence that the change from surplus to deficit occurred in 1977? After years of strong surplus in trade, it all changed only a few years after the removal of the gold standard. Here's what is troubling about all of this: Because the Fed is free to decide how much money to print up, it means that our ever-growing IOUs are becoming worth less and less. We buy more and more on credit, and our IOUs are piling up. The days when currency was backed by gold

are gone, and the United States has become a riverboat gambler, drunk and losing, demanding more and more credit to continue playing. Let's not overlook the historical reality: When the dollar's value falls, gold's value rises. As our trade deficit gets ever higher and as the Fed continues printing IOUs, the value begins to soften. The more currency put into circulation, the greater the dilution and the worse the situation becomes. But for the value of gold, this is good news.

2. *The budget deficit.* Where is the government getting all of that money it continues to spend? The $759 billion budget deficit is dependent on those incredibly low interest rates that are the centerpiece of the Fed's monetary policy. What happens when rates start to climb? Each year's deficit spending only adds to the national debt, and that means the budget itself sinks deeper and deeper into the hole. Who is going to make those interest payments in the future? The math is not encouraging. The higher the debt, the higher the interest. And the higher the interest rate, the greater the impact on the taxpayer (that would be you and me and our children).

3. *A limited world supply.* Gold is a limited commodity, unlike currency. As long as the Fed has access to printing presses, it is able to continue pumping adrenaline into the economy. But gold is *real* money in every sense, and its value is enhanced because there is only so much of it. This is the most important difference between currency and money. Now that we are off the gold standard, the Fed believes it can ignore currency valuation and continue on the "full faith and credit" system. As an investment, the dollar is becoming more and more suspect. In comparison, as dollar troubles get worse, the limited supply of gold will become more valuable. Cause and effect—that is what drives market values. Dollars fall, gold rises. It's unavoidable.

4. *The currency value of gold.* Most people can appreciate the difference between an IOU and actual money. If your boss handed you an IOU on payday, you would not be happy. You'd rather be able to cash a check and use the money. But in fact, the dollar *is* an IOU, and we're all trading these IOUs as currency without any real backing. We are going to see

an increasing trend among foreign central banks to buy gold in exchange for dollars. This gradually increasing demand for gold will have the unavoidable impact of increasing gold's market value. How high can it go? Only time will tell, but the weakening dollar is encouraging for the future market in gold.

THE DISMAL HISTORY OF PHONY MONEY

History has shown that money—not counterfeit, but *official* money printed by the government—has been known to lose value and become virtually worthless. Examples include Russian rubles from pre-Revolution days, 50-million marks from 1920s Germany, and Cuban pesos from pre-Castro days. In all of these cases, jarring political and economic change destroyed currency values—suddenly, completely, and permanently.

What kinds of events could do the same thing to the U.S. dollar, and what can you do today to position yourself strategically? The potential fall of the dollar is good news if you know what steps to take today. We're not as insulated as many Americans believe. In the 1930s, 20 percent of all U.S. banks went broke and 15 percent of life savings went up in smoke. After the emergency measures put into effect by President Franklin D. Roosevelt through the Emergency Banking Relief Act of 1933, confidence was restored with another piece of legislation: the 1933 Glass–Steagall Act. This bill created the Federal Deposit Insurance Corporation (FDIC), insuring all U.S. bank deposits against loss.

The severity of the growing situation had been seen well in advance. The financial newspaper *Barron's,* established in 1921, editorialized in 1933:

> Since early December, Washington had known that a major banking and financial crisis was probably inevitable. It was merely a question of where the first break would come and the manner of its coming.[2]

Two weeks earlier, the same column cautioned its readers that when the dollar begins to lose value, this leads to a series of "flights"—from property into bank deposits, then from deposits into currency, and finally from currency into gold.[3]

We can apply these astute observations from 1933 to today's currency situation. The government, anticipating a flight from currency into gold, had already made hoarding gold or even owning it illegal. The second step—insuring accounts in federal banks—helped to calm down the mood. By preventing the panic, these actions enabled the currency to be stabilized. But in those times, we were still on the gold standard. The currency in circulation was, in fact, backed by something. Remember, that riverboat gambler who keeps asking for ever-higher markers will eventually run out of credit. At some point the casino boss will realize that the gambler's ability to repay is questionable. Maybe those markers are just a heap of IOUs that can never be cashed in.

In the 1930s, the causes of the Great Depression were complex but related to a series of obvious abuses in monetary, financial, and banking policies. History has simplified the issue by blaming the Depression on the stock market crash. The stock market crash, one of many symptoms of policies run amok, has lessons for modern times. The unbridled printing of money—expansion of the IOU economy—is good news for those who recognize the potential for gold.

We hear experts on TV and in the print media shrugging off the deficit problems. "Our economy is strong and getting stronger" is the mantra of those with a vested interest in keeping dollars flowing: Wall Street brokers and analysts, for example. But we cannot ignore the facts. The federal deficit is growing by more than $40 billion per month. It is *not* realistic to point to this economy and say it's doing just fine.

Gold is the beneficiary of reckless monetary policies *and* the War on Terror. Check the average value of an ounce of gold over the past decade. It has been rising steadily since the end of 2001, jumping from $275.50 on November 30, 2001, to hit $783.50 on November 30, 2007, before going higher still, just a few weeks later, to $936. (See Figure 4.1.)

The cause of this change in gold's price may be attributed at least partly to the attack on the World Trade Center. But it reflects equally on the Fed's monetary policies and spiraling debt-based economic recovery. During the same period that gold prices have begun to rise,

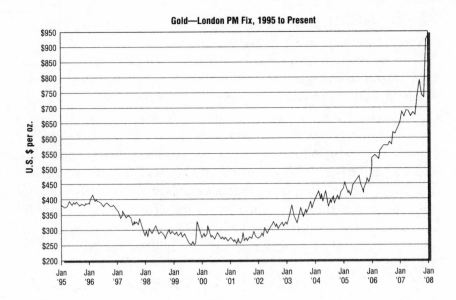

FIGURE 4.1   Gold, 1995–2008

we should also take a look at the trend in money in circulation. (See Figure 4.2.)

This is troubling for the dollar, but—again—great news for gold. Remember what the world economic and political situation was like in the early 1970s: a weakening dollar, easy money, and international unrest. Sound familiar? We're back in the same combination of circumstances that were present when gold prices went from $35 to over $850 per ounce in 1980. Since 1995, the value of currency in circulation has nearly doubled (up 95.7 percent); by 2006, the "phony money" pumped into the economy reached $783.5 billion. The Fed's policy sounds like a replay of that popular milk commercial: "Need money? We'll print more."

The numbers prove that gold is going to be the investment of the future. World mining in gold averages 80 million ounces per year, but demand has been running at 110 million ounces. So if central banks want to hold the value of gold steady, at least 30 million ounces per year must be sold into the market. This creates a squeeze. As the dollar weakens, central banks will want to increase their holdings in gold bullion, not sell it off. This is why gold's price has started to rise

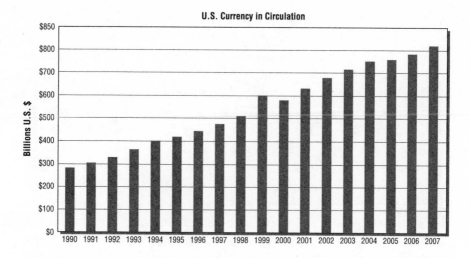

FIGURE 4.2 U.S. Currency in Circulation, 1990–2007
Source: Federal Reserve.

and must continue to rise into the future. As long as that demand grows—and it will rise as the dollar's value continues falling—the price of gold simply has to reflect the forces of supply and demand.

But, you might ask, why do central banks want to hold down the value of gold? We have to recognize how this whole money game works. Most world currencies are off the gold standard, following the U.S. example. So as gold's value rises, it competes with each country's currency. Of course, the trend toward weakening currencies and the continuing demand for gold mean that the growth in gold's value could continue strongly for many years to come.

SMOKE AND MIRRORS: THE TRAGIC FACTS ABOUT FIAT MONEY

When the United States removed its currency from the gold standard, it seemed to make economic sense at the time. President Nixon saw this as the solution to a range of economic problems and, combined with wage and price freezes, printing as much money as desired looked like a good idea. Unfortunately, most of the world's currencies followed suit. The world economy now runs primarily on a fiat money system.

Fiat money is so-called because it is not backed by any tangible asset such as gold, silver, or even seashells. The issuing government has decreed by fiat that "this money is a legal exchange medium, and it is worth what we say." So, lacking a gold backing or backing of some other precious metal, what gives the currency value? Is there a special reserve somewhere? No. Some economists have tried to explain away the problems of fiat money by pointing to the vast wealth of the United States in terms of productivity, natural resources, and land. But even if those assets are counted, they're not liquid. They're not part of the system of exchange. We have to deal with the fact that fiat money holds its value only as long as the people using that money continue to believe it has value—and as long as they continue to find people who will accept the currency in exchange for goods and services. The value of fiat money relies on confidence and expectation. So as we continue to increase twin deficit bubbles and as long as consumer debt keeps rising, our fiat money will eventually lose value. Gold, in comparison, has tangible value based on real market forces of supply and demand.

The short-term effect of converting from the gold standard to fiat money has been widespread prosperity. So the overall impression is that U.S. monetary policy has created and sustained this prosperity. Why abandon the dollar when times are so good?

This is where the great monetary trap is found. If we study the many economic bubbles in effect today, we know we eventually have to face up to the excesses, and that a big correction will occur. That means the dollar will fall and gold's value will rise as a direct result.

The sad lesson of economic history will be that when the gold standard is abandoned, and when governments can print too much money, they will. That tendency is a disaster for any economic system, because excess money in circulation (too much debt, in other words) only encourages consumer behavior mirroring that policy. Thus, we find ourselves in record-high levels of credit card debt, refinanced mortgages, and personal bankruptcies—all connected to that supposed prosperity based on printing far too much currency: the fiat system.

We can see where this overprinting will lead. As debt grows relative to gross domestic product (GDP), we would expect to see positive signs elsewhere, such as growth in new jobs. But like a Tiananmen Square Rolex watch deal, the value simply isn't there. There is some job growth, but, in reality, there is also a decline in earnings. High-paying manufacturing jobs have been replaced and exceeded by low-paying retail and health care sector jobs, so even if more people are at work, real earnings are down. Instead of simply measuring the number of jobs, an honest tracking system would also compare average wages and salaries in those jobs. Then we would be able to see what is really going on—more low-paying jobs being created, replacing high-paying jobs being lost.

THE NEW ROMAN EMPIRE

In 20 B.C., the Roman Emperor Augustus began printing money faster than gold production, even though he'd ordered gold mines to produce 24 hours per day in the outlying regions of the Empire. Future emperors followed the pattern, spending nonstop. Nero reduced the currency's value intentionally in order to continue spending, and ever-larger trade deficits resulted between Rome and its colonies and trading partners. Of course, these policies were part of the larger gradual decline of the Roman Empire.

History provides many examples along these lines. About 1,100 years ago, China issued paper money but eventually abandoned the practice because excessive currency in circulation caused inflation. When Spain found gold in Mexico in the sixteenth century, it became the world's richest nation. The Spanish used the gold to buy, buy, buy, and to expand their military influence. But the wars eventually used up their wealth, so Spain began issuing debt to pay the bills, leading of course to loss of its economic and military power. The French went through a similar period in the eighteenth century, printing way too much paper money and suffering unbelievable levels of inflation as a consequence.

President Abraham Lincoln authorized the use of paper currency with the Legal Tender Act. The result, once again, was runaway inflation. The debt financed the Civil War, but it created a widespread disdain for the practice, at least until 1913 when the Federal Reserve was created.

In the twentieth century, we saw many examples of monetary disasters. In Germany during the 1920s, war reparations destroyed the economy and large amounts of paper money were printed in an attempt to pay reparations (paying imposed debt with new debt). Of course, it didn't achieve anything but massive devaluation. In 1934, the United States joined the trend. Roosevelt set the value of gold at $35 per ounce in an attempt to end the Great Depression. And we know that, years later, Presidents Nixon and Ford completed the cycle of removal from the gold standard once and for all.

The effect has been worldwide, and it only makes the case for investing in gold more compelling. We see repeatedly from history that when countries are on the gold standard, they thrive—and when they go off the gold standard, that move leads to trouble. The problems seem to appear after 30 years. So if we count from the Nixon decision of 1971 to go off the gold standard, we should have seen problems soon after 2001. It was in 2002, in fact, when the value of gold started its current rise. So the 30 years of prosperity after removal of the gold standard have come to an end.

FIAT MONEY SYSTEMS OF THE PAST

A short trek along the dusty crossroads of history is all it takes to see that time and again when countries go off the gold standard, trouble ensues. The gold standard forces spending discipline on politicians, despots, demagogues, and democrats. When a country is on the gold standard, it has to live within its means. But when it goes off the gold standard and begins using fiat money, the sky's the limit.

That's when the trouble begins.

As long as a government—any government—is able to print money indefinitely, you can bet that it will. A government cannot be trusted to control its spending ways any more than a college freshman with dad's unlimited credit card during spring break. If the temptation is put out there, governments are going to go too far. Unfortunately, even the best economic experts can only identify when the printing of money has gone too far by one yardstick: when the system implodes. By then it's too late to prevent the damage.

Let's review some ill-fated historical examples.

The Roman Empire—In 20 B.C., Augustus ordered Gallic mines to operate around the clock to fund ever-growing infrastructure costs.

Even so, the Empire continued printing money beyond its reserves, causing inflation. The trend was followed by subsequent emperors until 64 A.D. when the infamous Nero cut back on the amount of silver in coins. Poor monetary policy coupled with abuses among the elite led to the eventual fall of the entire Empire.

China, Ninth Century A.D—A new innovation, paper money, came into being. It was described as "flying money" because a breeze could blow it out of a holder's hand. Originally meant as a temporary fix for a copper shortage, the paper money system got out of control. As one might predict, it was all too easy to just keep printing, which led to uncontrolled inflation. As bad an idea as it was, Marco Polo took some paper money back with him to Europe, where few people believed his tall tales of Chinese paper money. He described how seriously the Chinese took their paper money when he wrote:

> All these pieces of paper are issued with as much solemnity and authority as if they were pure gold or silver; and on every piece a variety of officials, whose duty it is, have to write their names, and to put their seals. And when all is duly prepared, the chief officer deputed by the Khan smears the Seal entrusted to him with vermilion, and impresses it on the paper, so that the form of the Seal remains printed upon it in red: the Money is then authentic. Anyone forging it would be punished with death.[4]

A few hundred years later, the Europeans were ready to take a shot at making their own solemn version of paper money.

Spain, Fifteenth Century—Spain grew to become the richest country in the world, based primarily on gold discoveries in Mexico. Spain, a country of contradictions, enjoyed growing wealth while running the infamous Spanish Inquisition, one of its darker moments. In 1481, Ferdinand and Isabella appointed the notorious inquisitor Tomás de Torquemada to run the show. So the availability of wealth led to colonial adventurism, social cruelty, and eventually excessive debt and national bankruptcy.

France, Eighteenth Century—John Law tried to revolutionize money and the way it was used. He said, "My secret is to make gold out of paper."[5] This early Western experiment with paper money has formed the basis of today's widespread currency systems. France, suffering from the abuses of the court of Louis XIV, had a nearly worthless coinage system. The king, during the last 14 years of his rule, spent two billion livres above tax collections. Law's idea to fix the problem was to create notes (paper money) to facilitate trade. By 1717, Law had put an elaborate Ponzi scheme into play. He promised riches to anyone who invested in his private bank. The government granted him exclusive rights to control the currency, print money, control sea trade, and administer revenues from tobacco, salt, and the exaggerated riches of France's newest colony, Louisiana. Speculation accelerated and, by 1720, the scheme began falling apart. Before it was over, the paper money lost 90 percent of its face value. Law died in 1729 and an epitaph was published that year in France: "Here lies that celebrated Scotsman, that peerless mathematician who, by the rules of algebra, sent France to the poorhouse."[6]

United States, Eighteenth Century—By 1764, the United States was plagued by a volume of worthless notes. Issued during the French and Indian War, these notes brought about a widespread economic recession. Britain declared that the Colonies were no longer allowed to issue drafts or paper money. During the Revolutionary War, Congress authorized paper money to be printed. This so-called continental money was supposed to be backed by gold and silver, and each state promised to provide a share of bullion reserves as collateral. But it never happened and, predictably, continental money was printed with no backing. Making matters worse, the British subverted the effort by counterfeiting their own version of the bills. The money became worthless and by 1780 anything of little value was described as being "not worth a continental."[7] Finally, in 1781, continentals could be redeemed for newly issued Treasury notes. The new superintendent of finance, Robert Morris, issued these and they became known as "Morris notes." They were redeemable in hard currency at a date noted on the bills, but, lacking any real reserves, these notes also declined in value.[8]

France, Eighteenth Century, Part II—France had been deceived by John Law and his currency magic, but didn't learn from the lesson. By 1791, France was ready to try paper currency again. The government, in anti-aristocracy mode, confiscated property and other assets from the wealthy in exchange for *assignats,* notes that paid interest, operating like land mortgage notes. Far from solving the problem of

A NEW SHAYS' REBELLION?

In January 1787, Daniel Shays, a former officer in the Revolutionary Army, led 2,000 farmers in a revolt against U.S. government troops at a Springfield, Massachusetts, armory. The rebels, mostly farmers, were protesting serious economic conditions, the worst of which was the lack of a stable currency. They demanded that the government create what they called "sound money." In other words, the farmers were demanding a gold-backed dollar. There was a lot of money in circulation, but very little of it was worth its face value.

The 2,000 rebels were arrested and the leaders were given death sentences, but all were later pardoned. This was an early and relatively small example of what can happen when a country does not have sound money.

The farmers who followed Daniel Shays knew that their economic survival depended on fixing the problem. Their actions forced the government to create a single currency and control it. Now, more than 200 years later, we face a similar problem but on a far larger scale. Physical rebellion is not the solution today; but many serious problems remain: unfair and inconsistent taxation, expensive lawsuits, and excessively high salaries for government cronies. Sound familiar? These were among the complaints that led to Shays' Rebellion.

economic disparity among the classes, the extreme measures only made matters worse. Within four years, inflation had risen by 13,000 percent. Few instruments have declined to zero value as quickly as the *assignats*. In a foreword to a book on the historical implications of French monetary policy, John Mackay described France's attempts at a fiat money system as

> the most gigantic attempt ever made in the history of the world by a government to create an inconvertible paper currency, and to maintain its circulation at various levels of value. It also records what is perhaps the greatest of all government efforts . . . to enact and enforce a legal limit of commodity prices. Every fetter that could hinder the will or thwart the wisdom of democracy had been

shattered. . . . But the attempts failed. They left behind them a
legacy of moral and material desolation and woe.[9]

Argentina, Nineteenth and Twentieth Centuries—Perhaps learning
from the mistakes of the Europeans, Argentina went on the gold standard in 1853. For the next century, the economy thrived. In 1943,
Juan Peron's coup destroyed the country's system and gold reserves
disappeared, to be replaced by paper money. This began a downward-
spiraling economy that has only recently begun to recover.

United States, Nineteenth Century—During the Civil War, President
Lincoln authorized issuance of paper money to help finance the war
effort. The resulting inflation caused a public sentiment against paper
money that lasted until 1913, when the Federal Reserve System was
devised.

Germany, Twentieth Century—In 1923, the so-called Weimar
Republic—a post–World War I temporary government—had to deal
with repressive war reparations. It began printing massive amounts of
paper money to make payments, to the extent that the currency
became completely worthless. The devastation paved the way for the
Nazi movement of the late 1920s and early 1930s, and directly to
World War II.

United States, Twentieth Century—The United States has removed
itself from the gold standard in the most recent switch to a fiat money
system. This took place in three phases. First, in 1934, President
Roosevelt declared that an ounce of gold was to be valued at $35, up
from its previous level of $20.67. The hope was that this change
would end the Depression. Second, the Bretton Woods system agreed
upon in 1944 (explained at the beginning of this book) achieved
worldwide agreement to peg currencies to gold. But in practice, the
U.S. dollar became an international currency and other countries
pegged their currencies to the dollar. Bretton Woods also opened the
door to widespread use of debt (i.e., printing of additional currency
above gold reserves) to facilitate international trade. Third, in 1971,
President Nixon ended convertibility of dollars to gold. The United
States had already been printing paper money far above reserve levels;
this removal from the gold standard destroyed the Bretton Woods
Agreement, creating a worldwide gold drain.

BRETTON WOODS

The year was 1944. For the first time in modern history, an international agreement was reached to govern monetary policy among nations. It was, significantly, a chance to create a stabilizing international currency and ensure monetary stability once and for all. In total, 730 delegates from 44 nations met for three weeks in July that year at a hotel resort in Bretton Woods, New Hampshire.

It was a significant opportunity, but it fell short of what could have been achieved. It was a turning point in monetary history, however.

The result of this international meeting, the Bretton Woods Agreement, had the original purpose of rebuilding after World War II through a series of currency stabilization programs and infrastructure loans to war-ravaged nations. By 1946, the system was in full operation through the newly established International Bank for Reconstruction and Development (IBRD, the World Bank) and the International Monetary Fund (IMF).

What makes the Bretton Woods accords so interesting to us today is the fact that the whole plan for international monetary policy was based on nations agreeing to adhere to a global *gold* standard. Each country signing the agreement promised to maintain its currency at values within a narrow margin to the value of gold. The IMF was established to facilitate payment imbalances on a temporary basis.

This system worked for 25 years. But it was flawed in its underlying assumptions. By pegging international currency to gold at $35 an ounce, it failed to take into consideration the change in gold's actual value since 1934, when the $35 level had been set. The dollar had lost substantial purchasing power during and after World War II, and as European economies built back up, the ever-growing drain on U.S. gold reserves doomed the Bretton Woods Agreement as a permanent, working system. This problem was described by a former senior vice president of the Federal Reserve Bank of New York:

> From the very beginning, gold was the vulnerable point of the Bretton Woods system. Yet the open-ended gold commitment assumed by the United States government under the Bretton Woods legislation is readily understandable in view of the extraordinary

circumstances of the time. At the end of the war, our gold stock amounted to $20 billion, roughly 60 percent of the total of official gold reserves. As late as 1957, United States gold reserves exceeded by a ratio of three to one the total dollar reserves of all the foreign central banks. The dollar bestrode the exchange markets like a colossus.[10]

In 1971, experiencing accelerating depletion of its gold reserves, the United States removed its currency from the gold standard, and Bretton Woods was no longer workable.

In some respects, the ideas behind Bretton Woods were much like an economic United Nations. The combination of the worldwide depression of the 1930s and the Second World War were key in leading so many nations to an economic summit of such magnitude.

The opinion of the day was that trade barriers and high costs had caused the worldwide depression, at least in part. Also, during that time it was common practice to use currency devaluation as a means for affecting neighboring countries' imports *and* reducing payment deficits. Unfortunately, the practice led to chronic deflation, unemployment, and a reduction in international trade. The lessons learned in the 1930s (but subsequently forgotten by many nations) included a realization that the use of currency as a tactical economic tool invariably causes more problems than it solves.

The situation was summed up well by Cordell Hull, U.S. secretary of state from 1933 through 1944, who wrote:

> Unhampered trade dovetailed with peace; high tariffs, trade barriers, and unfair economic competition, with war. . . . If we could get a freer flow of trade . . . so that one country would not be deadly jealous of another and the living standards of all countries might rise, thereby eliminating the economic dissatisfaction that breeds war, we might have a reasonable chance of lasting peace.[11]

Hull's suggestion that war often has an economic root is reasonable given the position of both Germany and Japan in the 1930s. The trade embargo imposed by the United States against Japan, specifically intended to curtail Japanese expansion, may have been a leading cause for Japan's militaristic stance.

Another observer agreed, saying that poor economic relations among nations "inevitably result in economic warfare that will be but a prelude and instigator of military warfare on an even vaster scale."[12]

Bretton Woods had the original intention of smoothing out economic conflict, in recognition of the problems that economic disparity causes. The nations at the meeting knew that these economic problems were at least partly to blame for the war itself, and that economic reform would help to prevent future wars. At that time, the United States was without any doubt the most powerful nation in the world, both militarily and economically. Because the fighting did not take place on U.S. soil, the country built up its industrial might during the war, selling weapons to its allies while developing its own economic strength. Manufacturing by 1945 was twice the annual rate of 1935–1939.[13]

Due to its economic dominance, the United States held the leadership role at Bretton Woods. It is also important to note that the United States owned 80 percent of the world's gold reserves at the time.[14] So the United States had every motive to agree to the use of the gold standard to organize world currencies and to create and encourage free trade. The gold standard evolved over a period of hundreds of years, planned by a central bank, government, or committee of business leaders.

Throughout most of the nineteenth century, the gold standard dominated currency exchange. Gold created a fixed exchange rate between nations. Money supply was limited to gold reserves, so nations lacking gold were required to borrow money to finance their production and investment.

When the gold standard was in force, it was true that the net sum of trade surplus and deficit came out to zero overall, because accounts were eventually settled in gold—and credit was limited as well. In comparison, in today's fiat money system, it is not gold but *credit* that determines how much money a country can spend. So instead of economic might being dictated by gold reserves, it is dictated by a country's borrowing power. The trade deficit and the trade surplus are only in balance in theory, because the disparity between the two sides is funded with debt.

The pegged rates—the value of currency to the value of gold— maintained sensible economic policy based on a nation's productivity and gold reserves. Following Bretton Woods, the pegged rate was formalized by agreement among the leading economic powers of the world.

The concept was a good one. However, in practice the international currency naturally became the U.S. dollar, and other nations pegged their currencies to the dollar rather than to the value of gold. The actual outcome of Bretton Woods was to replace the gold standard with the dollar standard. Once the United States linked the dollar to gold at a value of $35 per ounce, the whole system fell into place, at least for a while. Since the dollar was convertible to gold and other nations pegged their currencies to the dollar, it created a pseudo-gold standard.

The British economist John Maynard Keynes represented Great Britain at Bretton Woods. Keynes preferred establishing a system that would have encouraged economic growth rather than a gold-pegged system. He favored creation of an international central bank and possibly even a world currency. He proposed that the goal of the conference was "to find a common measure, a common standard, a common rule acceptable to each and not irksome to any."[15]

Keynes' ideas were not accepted. The United States, in its leading economic position, preferred the plan offered by its representative, Harry Dexter White. The U.S. position was intended to create and maintain price stability rather than outright economic growth. As a consequence, Third World progress would be achieved through lending and infrastructure investment through the IMF, which was charged with managing trade deficits to avoid currency devaluation. In joining the IMF, each country was assigned a trade quota to fund the international effort, budgeted originally at $8.8 billion. Disparity among countries was to be managed through a series of borrowings. A country could borrow from the IMF, which would be acting in fact like a central bank.

The Bretton Woods Agreement did not include any provisions for creation of reserves. The presumption was that gold production would be sufficient to continue funding growth and that any short-term problems could be resolved through the borrowing regimens. Anticipating a high volume of demand for such lending in reconstruction efforts after World War II, the Bretton Woods attendees formed the IBRD, providing an additional $10 billion to be paid by member nations.

As well-intentioned as the idea was, the agreements and institutions that grew from Bretton Woods were not adequate for the economic problems of postwar Europe. The United States was experiencing huge trade surplus years while carrying European war debt. U.S. reserves were huge and growing each year.

By 1947, it became clear that the IMF and IBRD were not going to fix the problems of European postwar economic woes. To help address the issue, the United States set up a system to help finance recovery among European countries. The European Recovery Program (better known as the Marshall Plan) was organized to give grants to countries to rebuild. The problems of European nations, according to Secretary of State George Marshall, "are so much greater than her present ability to pay that she must have substantial help or face economic, social, and political deterioration of a very grave character."[16]

Between 1948 and 1954, the United States gave 16 Western European nations $17 billion in grants. Believing that former enemies Japan and Germany would provide markets for future U.S. exports, policies were enacted to encourage economic growth. During this period, the Cold War became increasingly worse as the arms race continued. The USSR had signed the Bretton Woods Agreement, but it refused to join or participate in the IMF. Thus, the proposed economic reforms turned into part of the struggle between capitalism and Communism on the world stage.

It became increasingly difficult to maintain the peg of the U.S. dollar to $35-per-ounce gold. An open market in gold continued in London, and crises affected the going value of gold. The conflict between the fixed price of gold between central banks at $35 per ounce and open market value depended on the moment. During the Cuban missile crisis, for example, the open market value of gold was $40 per ounce. The mood among U.S. leaders began moving away from belief in the gold standard.

President Lyndon B. Johnson argued in 1967:

The world supply of gold is insufficient to make the present system workable—particularly as the use of the dollar as a reserve currency is essential to create the required international liquidity to sustain world trade and growth.[17]

By 1968, Johnson had enacted a series of measures designed to curtail the outflow of U.S. gold. Even so, on March 17, 1968, a run on gold closed the London Gold Pool permanently. By this time, it had become clear that maintaining the gold standard under the Bretton Woods configuration was no longer practical. Either the monetary system had to change or the gold standard itself would need to be revised.

During this period, the IMF set up Special Drawing Rights (SDRs) for use as trade between countries. The intention was to create a type of paper gold system, while taking pressure off the United States to continue serving as central banker to the world. However, this did not solve the problem; the depletion of U.S. gold reserves continued until 1971. By that time, the U.S. dollar was overvalued in relation to gold reserves. The United States held only 22 percent gold coverage of foreign reserves by that year.

Special Drawing Rights acted as a basket of key national currencies to facilitate the inevitable trade imbalances. However, Bretton Woods lacked any effective mechanism for checking reserve growth. Only gold and the U.S. asset were considered seriously as reserves, but gold production was lagging. Accordingly, dollar reserves had to expand to make up the difference in lagging gold availability, causing a growing U.S. current account deficit. The solution, it was hoped, would be the SDR.

While these instruments continue to exist, this long-term effectiveness can only be the subject of speculation. Today SDRs make up 3 percent of IMF members' nongold reserves—three times the holdings in 2005. In 1971, when the United States went off the gold standard, Bretton Woods ceased to function as an effective centralized monetary body. In theory, SDRs—used today on a very limited scale of transactions between the IMF and its members—could function as the beginnings of an international currency. But given the widespread use of the U.S. dollar as the peg for so many currencies worldwide, it is unlikely that such a shift to a new direction will occur before circumstances make it the only choice.

The Bretton Woods system collapsed, partially due to economic expansion in excess of the gold standard's funding abilities on the part of the United States and other member nations. However, the problems of currency systems *not* pegged to gold lead to economic problems far worse.

THE GREAT DOLLAR STANDARD ERA

The fiat money system in effect in the United States today makes this point. It may be interesting to note that today many economists fear that a *return* to the gold standard or institution of an international monetary system could actually trigger a depression—a collapse of the financial economy. One author made an attempt to tie the Great Depression to England's attempt to return to the gold standard in the 1920s.[18] However, most historians would agree that trying to go back to the gold standard was not actually the cause of the worldwide depression. The cause was more likely out-of-control credit resulting from suspension of the gold standard. The global economy was in trouble at least a full decade prior to England's change in monetary policy.

However, the book made a good point: It is no simple matter to revert to a more sensible standard. Consequences are inevitable. It would not be easy for the major currencies to return to an organized Bretton Woods Agreement type of system. Growth has occurred at such an accelerated pace that an attempt to return to the gold standard in one move would not work. This does not mean that the fiat money system can succeed. To the contrary, no such system has in the past.

No fiat money system has ever succeeded. History has shown time and again that eventually excessive government spending makes paper money worthless. Today, the common belief among U.S. economists and the Federal Reserve is that consumption is the fix-all. The fact that consumption is taking place with borrowed money does not seem to matter. So consumer debt, national budget deficits, and trade gaps have become a sort of norm, whereas in the past all of these economic trends were viewed as early warning signs of a weakening currency.

An argument against the gold standard is based on gold's rarity. We cannot expect any economic expansion as long as we are held back by a commodity in limited supply, the argument goes. However, the argument is flawed.

Supply and demand alter the value of every commodity in an efficient economic system. As demand increases for a unit of exchange (i.e., gold), the price rises. This is an efficient system. Demand pushes the price up, and supply pushes the price down. When paper money is in use, the whole efficiency of the economic system goes out the window. As long as the government can print more money, it can continue to expand a consumption base in spite of any supply and demand, and in spite of the limited supply of gold itself.

Eventually, though, all of that printed money exceeds its own life cycle. It becomes worthless, as we have seen time and again—in Rome, China, Spain, France, Germany, and now the United States.

Perhaps a paper money system pegged specifically to commodity reserves would give the currency the stability it needs and rein in government spending. We don't pretend to know the solution to a runaway fiat regime. But experience tells us that governments have less discipline than a hungry fat man at an all-you-can-eat buffet. They are simply going to print, print, print, until the system fails. Is this a matter of weak character or simply human nature? Some, like Clif Droke, have argued that governments "must be composed of men of the highest moral standing, and ideally should be Christian in composition."[19] Who is going to decide what constitutes the highest morals, and what track record gives Christians a monopoly on integrity?

The monetary system is evolving before our very eyes. Never before in human history has the reserve currency of the world been so burdened with debt. And never has the transfer of one international currency to another been peaceful. Is the euro likely to supplant the dollar as international money?[20] Perhaps it will be the Chinese yuan.

During debate on the Bretton Woods Agreement, John Maynard Keynes hinted at the desirability of a world central banking system and a world currency. We have not had such a system since the sixth century, when the Roman coin the solidus (originally minted by Emperor Constantine) was "accepted everywhere from end to end of the earth."[21] The solidus was respected for centuries, while it also competed with the dinar in the Moslem world. Both coins held their value for good reason: The metallic content of these coins remained consistent over time, and robust economic activity spread their use throughout the known world.

Both coins lost value in about the nineteenth century, and for the same reason: reduction of metallic weight. In an effort to stretch currency values, rulers reduced weight, causing debasement and, eventually, loss of trust in the market. The introduction of inferior-grade coins further accelerated the debasement of the traditional solidus and dinar.[22]

The next go-round of worldwide coinage occurred in the thirteenth century. In Italy, the *genoin* (introduced in Genoa) and the *florin* (from Florence) became true world currencies during a period of expanding international trade. Two hundred years later, the system expanded with introduction of the *ducato* in Venice.[23]

These coins held steady in value until the fifteenth century, when silver mining in several European countries changed valuation of metals. It is interesting to note that debasement of these currencies was not accompanied by inflation. This was due to the fact that as money supplies grew, so did real output and production. By today's standards, it was a minuscule economy, but the model made the point concerning valuation of currency-based monetary systems and their relationship with production and consumption.

The characteristics that made older international monetary systems stable included high unitary value; intrinsic stability; and strong economic trade, production, and balance of consumption.[24] A fourth attribute is widespread acceptance of a currency as a means of acceptable monetary value.

In comparison to modern fiat money systems, these attributes become significant. We can judge the actual health of a monetary system by comparing its attributes to these older international systems. An argument made by U.S. economists and the chairman of the Federal Reserve is that the United States does, indeed, enjoy all of those attributes in its monetary system. But the various consumption bubbles that control the U.S. economy belie this opinion. In fact, we may be on the verge of seeing the dollar being replaced gradually by another medium, perhaps the euro. The study of history has shown:

> A series of international monies has existed historically, each occupying center stage sometimes for several centuries and eventually being replaced by the next. The only exception is the dollar, which is the current international money and, therefore, has not been replaced. . . . The euro area is large enough in terms of trade to be a serious competitor to the dollar as an international money.[25]

The solution, ultimately, to the problem of governmental abuse of its printing presses is to establish a modern-day international currency. The U.S. dollar has served as a de facto international currency for many years, and arguments are being made in support of the euro taking its place. However, true reform would require that an international currency have the backing and stability of gold reserves. The fiat system has never worked, and today's fiat money will not work permanently, either.

A MODERN DILEMMA

The Great Dollar Standard Era is a direct result of the removal of gold as the underpinning of the world's currencies. The vast overprinting of currency will inevitably debase the value of the U.S. dollar and, because so many foreign currencies are pegged to the dollar, the currency of those nations as well. Fiat money, simply put, is created out of nothing. A future promise to pay has never supported monetary value for long, and the United States is so overextended today that it is doubtful it could ever honor its overall real debts. Counting obligations under Medicare and Social Security, the real debt of the United States is now approaching six times the reported national debt, estimates David Walker, former head of the GAO, now president and CEO of the newly founded Peter G. Peterson Foundation:

> Federal debt managed by the bureau [Bureau of the Public Debt] totaled about $9 billion at the end of fiscal year 2007. However, that number excludes many items, including the gap between scheduled and funded Social Security and Medicare benefits, veterans' health care, and a range of other commitments and contingencies that the federal government has pledged to support. If these items are factored in, the total burden in present federal dollars is estimated to be about $53 trillion. Stated differently, the estimated current total burden for every American is nearly $175,000; and every day that burden becomes larger.[26]

The argument favoring the current fiat system is that the demand for it grew out of barter, the need to facilitate ever-higher volumes of trade. If this were true, there would be a reasonable expectation that a system of paper drafts would make sense. But the reality is that fiat money has not grown out of barter, but from the previous gold standard. Given the lack of control over how much fiat money is placed in circulation—after all, it is based on nothing—we can only expect that the currency will continue to lose value over time. The model of fiat money is supported and defended with arguments that consumption is good for the economy, even with the use of vacant monetary systems. But there is a problem:

> The predictions of these models are at odds with the historical evidence. Fiat money did not in fact evolve . . . by means of a great leap forward from barter. Nor did fiat monies ever emerge out of thin air. Instead, fiat monies have always developed out of some previously existing money.[27]

Can we equate the problems inherent in fiat money with the effects of inflation? We have all heard that saving for retirement today is problematical because by the time we retire we will need more dollars to pay for the things we will need. By definition, this sounds like the consequences of inflation. But inflation is not simply higher prices; it has another aspect, which is devalued currency. We have to pay higher prices in the future because the currency is worth less relative to other currencies. That is the real inflation. Higher prices are only symptoms following the debasement of currency. If we examine *why* those prices go up, we discover that the reason is not necessarily corporate greed, inefficiency, or foreign price gouging. At the end of the day, it is the gradual loss of purchasing power, the need for more dollars to buy the same things. That's inflation. And fiat money is at the root of the problem.

The intrinsic problem with fiat money systems is how it unravels the basic economic reality. We know that it requires work to create real wealth. We labor and we are paid. We save and we earn interest. Government, however, produces nothing to create wealth, so it creates wealth out of an arbitrary system: fiat money. The problem is described well in the following passage:

> It takes work to create wealth. "Dollars" are created without any work—how much more work is involved in printing a $100 bill as compared to a $1 bill? Not only are ordinary people at home being deceived, but foreigners who accept and save our "dollars" in exchange for their goods and services are also being cheated.[28]

So are we "cheated" by the fiat money system? Under one interpretation, we have to contend with the reality that the dollar is not backed by anything of value. But as long as we all agree to assign value to the dollar, and as long as foreign central banks do the same, isn't it okay to use a fiat money system?

The problem becomes severe when, unavoidably, the system finally collapses. At some point, the Federal Reserve—with blessings of the Congress and the administration—prints and places so much money into circulation that its perceived value just evaporates. Can this happen? It has always happened in the past when fiat money systems were put into use. We have to wonder whether FDR was sincere when, in 1933, he declared that the currency had adequate backing. It wasn't until the following year that the president raised the ounce value of gold from $20.67 to $35. He explained his own monetary policy in 1933 after declaring the government's sole right to possess gold:

> More liberal provision has been made for banks to borrow on these assets at the Reserve Banks and more liberal provision has also been made for issuing currency on the security of those good assets. This currency is not fiat currency. It is issued on adequate security, and every good bank has an abundance of such security.[29]

It was the plan of the day. First, the law required that all citizens turn over their gold to the government. Second, the *value* of that gold was raised nearly 70 percent to $35 per ounce (after collecting it from the people, of course). Third, the president declared that currency printing was being liberalized—but it is backed by gold, so it's not a fiat system. This may have been true in 1933, but since then—having removed ourselves from the gold standard—the presses are printing money late into the night. The gold standard has been long forgotten in Congress, the Federal Reserve, and the executive branch.

THE POLITICS OF THE ECONOMY

It may be the view of some people that a perfect monetary system may include changes in value based on purchasing power and on the demand for money itself. Thus, rich nations would become richer and control the cost of goods, while poor nations would remain poor. In spite of the best efforts under the Bretton Woods Agreement, it has proven impossible to simply let money find its own level of value. Unlike stocks and real estate, the free market does not work well with monetary value because each country has its own self-interests. Furthermore, today's post–Bretton Woods monetary system has no method available to prevent or mitigate trade imbalances. Thus, trade surplus versus deficit continues to expand out of control. The United States ended up accumulating current account deficits totaling more than $3 trillion between 1980 and 2000. This perverse twist on world money has had a strange effect:

> These deficits have acted as an economic subsidy to the rest of the world, but they have also flooded the world with dollars, which have replaced gold as the new international reserve asset. These deficits have, in effect, become the font of a new global money supply.[30]

This is what occurs when international money supplies become unregulated. We need a firmly controlled world banking system if only to stop the unending printing of money. If, indeed, U.S. deficits continue as a form of subsidy to the rest of the world, that can only lead to a worldwide economic collapse like the one seen in the 1920s and 1930s.

If it were possible to create a controlled international monetary unit, its effectiveness would demand ongoing regulation to prevent the disparities among nations with varying resources and reserves. Ludwig von Mises, noted twentieth-century economist, wrote:

> The idea of a money with an exchange value that is not subject to variations due to changes in the ratio between the supply of money and the need for it . . . demands the intervention of a regulatory authority in the determination of the value of money; and its continued intervention.[31]

Mises concluded that this need for intervention was itself a problem. It is unlikely that any governments would be trustworthy enough to properly ensure a *fair* valuation of money, were it left up to them; instead, governments are more likely than not to fall into the common fiat trap. Without limitations on how much money can be printed, it is human and governmental nature to print as much as possible. Mises observed that fiat money leads to monetary policy designed to achieve political aims:

> The state should at least refrain from exerting any sort of influence on the value of money. A metallic money, the augmentation or diminution of the quantity of metal available which is independent of deliberate human intervention, is becoming the modern monetary ideal.[32]

To an extent, the enactment of a fiat money system is likely either to be politically motivated or to soon become a political tool in the hands of government. We have to see how government attempts to influence economic health through a variety of means and in tandem with Federal Reserve policy: raising and lowering interest rates, enacting tax incentives for certain groups, legislating tax cuts or tax increases, and imposing or reducing trade restrictions or tariffs. All of these moves invariably have a pro and con argued politically rather than economically. The argument in modern-day U.S. politics is between Republican desires to reduce taxes as a means of stimulating growth versus Democratic views that we cannot afford tax cuts and such cuts are given to favored upper-income taxpayers. The arguments are complex and endless, but they are not just political tools; they are part of overall monetary and economic policy trends as well.

This has become our modern entry in the history of money. The belief on the part of government, rooted in an arrogant thinking that *power* extends even to the valuation of goods and services and monetary exchange, has led to a monetary policy that makes utterly no sense in historical perspective. Having gone over entirely to a fiat standard, government has chosen to ignore history and those market forces that ultimately decide the question of valuation, in spite of anything government does. This has always been true, as Jeffrey M. Herbener observed:

> The use of the precious metals was historically the choice of the market. Without interference from governments, traders adopted the parallel standard using gold and silver as money.[33]

If monetary policy were left alone and allowed to function in the free market, what would happen? Perhaps governments ultimately do follow the market by adopting the gold standard, as we have seen repeatedly in history: going on the gold standard, moving to fiat money, experiencing a debasement, and then returning to the gold standard. Herbener continued by observing:

> The fly in the ointment of the classical gold standard was precisely that since it was created and maintained by governments, it could be abandoned and destroyed by them. As the ideological tide turned against laissez-faire in favor of statism, governments intent upon expanding the scope of their interference in and control of the market economy found it necessary to eliminate the gold standard.[34]

Today, we live with that legacy. While historians marvel at the "end of history" and the triumph of free market economics, the Fed maintains "price controls" on the very symbol of economic freedom—the U.S. dollar itself.

CHAPTER 5

THE HELICOPTER THEORY, INFLATION, AND THE MONEY IN YOUR WALLET

The U.S. government has a technology, called a printing press, that allows it to produce as many U.S. dollars as it wishes at essentially no cost.

—Ben Bernanke

Of all the contrivances for cheating the laboring classes of mankind, none has been more effective than that which deludes them with paper money.

—Daniel Webster

On November 21, 2002, then Federal Reserve Governor Ben Bernanke gave an address before the National Economists Club in Washington, D.C. The speech has come to be known as "The Helicopter Theory" speech—in which Bernanke outlined an economic recipe to avert Japan-style deflation in the United States through a series of tax cuts and low interest rates that could effectively drop cash into the hands of consumers, as if from a helicopter. The result: inflation. Problem solved.

If you listen to Bernanke and company today, they are still patting themselves on the back. In their view, when consumers refinance their homes and increase their mortgage debt, that frees up money. That money is used to spend and, according to the Fed chairman, that is a good thing—even though the U.S. consumer savings rate has now dropped below zero.

The economy and its growing deficits can be predicted by looking at a parallel situation in the late 1990s in one of our Asian trade partners. Japan, with its work ethic and competitive spirit, discovered the hard way that deficit spending is not the way to grow an economy. It is, however, a good way to destroy it.

JAPAN: A CASE IN PERSPECTIVE

Indeed, we would be wise to heed the lessons of the Japanese experience.[1] We can learn a great deal about what is happening to our dollar today by reviewing the details of the "yen miracle."

In 1997, Japan went through an experience that proves the economic wisdom that weak economies have weak currencies and strong economies have strong currencies. This may seem obvious, but we see over and over that economists do not always accept this wisdom. While Greenspan, then our Fed head, said he was concerned with the possible connection between a weakened U.S. dollar and the prospects for the overall economy, his actions weren't convincing.

Myth versus the Real Japanese Experience

What the Japan experience showed was that when a country's economy is weakened, it doesn't take much to push it over the edge. After years of growth in its gross domestic product (GDP), the numbers began slowing down. This slowdown was tied to ever-higher budget deficits, so that by 1997 Japan was in trouble. That year, the government made modest cuts to its budget deficit, and the result was an economic free fall in 1998. Gross domestic product fell, inflation followed, and productivity slowed. In response, the government instituted record levels of deficit spending in a Greenspan-esque hope that deficit spending would fix a failing economy. But that same year, the Japanese economy, by all measurements, just got worse and worse.

By 1999, according to the Organization for Economic Cooperation and Development (OECD), restructuring was being promoted as fortification for the Japanese economy, but its effect would be doubtful:

> Firms have been making claims that they intend to . . . restructure their businesses. The number of restructuring announcements has surged. . . . But there is a legitimate concern . . . whether [restructuring will be] carried out . . . or whether [share buybacks] are being trotted out for the hoped-for favorable effect on the share price. . . . Many restructuring announcements lack any target for cost cutting by which they can be judged.[2]

As a matter of fact, it's doubtful that this attempt at restructuring was really helpful to the Japanese economy. It has not grown its way out of its economic and financial imbalances. In fact, the various financial stimulus packages have been ineffective. Between 1992 and 1999, the Japanese government launched 10 such packages, but during the same period its debt grew by $1.13 trillion. The Japanese government policy was premised on the idea that it is possible to spend a country's way out of economic trouble. The numbers prove this theory wrong.

The ratio of government debt to GDP soared from about 60 percent in 1992 to 105 percent of GDP in 1999. That is troubling for any economy involved in trade, such as Japan, China, or the United States. The Japanese history lesson reveals that you can't spend your way out of trouble. We can only hope that Mr. Bernanke is paying attention.

Even so, the theme—the official story, if you will—was that Japan's restructuring has fixed the problem. Many of those once-popular international mutual funds bought the story and went through a transitional period, moving investment dollars out of Europe and into Japan. We saw once again—as we have seen so many times in our own domestic stock market—an institutional herd mentality. If everyone is investing in Japan, we can't ignore it. We have to be there, too.

Selling business restructuring as the fix was effective, at least in terms of raising foreign investment levels. But restructuring is not the same as investment. Moving debt around and changing its face doesn't fix the problem of deficit spending—a fact the U.S. Fed has not yet learned. We may read all about Japan's promising plans for improving its economy, but the numbers don't support the claimed successes.

The chronic budget deficits coupled with very low interest rates held back any prospects of a real recovery. In fact, conditions in Japan during the 1990s were very similar to conditions in the United States today—and it's a mistake for U.S. policy makers to believe that we are immune from the same outcome that Japan has experienced.

We face an enigma in the case of Japan. Its economy is weak and remains chronically so, even though on the management side Japanese business cannot be blamed. The country has seen strong GDP growth, low inflation, and climbing exports. The economic fundamental indicators are positive as well: a very high savings rate, strong balance of payments, and virtually no inflation. Even so, Japan's economy refuses to jump-start. Why?

To understand what is going on in Japan—and by association, what may take place in the United States—it's helpful to compare Japan in the 1990s to the United States before the crash of 1929. The question is debated even today: Was the collapse of the market and of the 1929 economy inevitable? We know of the economic, business, and market excesses of the 1920s, so the unregulated environment was one possible culprit. But was there more? Was the market crash (and the depression that followed) the result of U.S. monetary policies before, during, or after the crash? Could looser money policies have avoided the economic problems?

Probably not.

From a monetary perspective, Japan is the greatest paradox in the world—strong indicators, but a chronically weak economy. Compare this to the United States, where our ever-falling economic indicators have not affected our dollar's value except gradually. Japan has the lowest interest rates of any industrialized nation, nearly zero; yet credit growth is the slowest in the world. Is this sluggish expansion a cause or effect of the economy's doldrums? It appears to be more effect than cause.

It remains troubling, however. In the face of chronic budget deficits, Japan has not been able to fix its economic pace. The economic policies and business practices are sound, investment and savings rates are high, and exports are surplus. Perhaps Japan's deficits simply got too large and all of the other economic positive signs simply haven't been enough to fix the budget problem. So what does this mean for the United States, where consumer credit increases every year at ever-faster rates, trade deficits are higher than ever, federal budget deficits are climbing, and, not surprisingly, the dollar is getting weaker and weaker each quarter?

DOOMSDAY? THE PROSPECT OF A MONETARY CRASH

The future for the U.S. dollar is the most important concern for the world economy, and for investors.[3] This is not merely Yankee arrogance; so many economies outside of the United States are pegged to the dollar or depend on its value to support their own economic health.

This is of great and immediate concern because, while the dollar has been slipping only gradually in the recent past, the rate of decline has picked up momentum. A dollar crash will have disastrous implications for global financial markets. At the end of 2001, the euro was worth $0.8915, but it has been on a steady upward march since then. On the last trading day of the third quarter in 2007, the euro hit a high of 1.4282. A target of 1.50 is very much within range. The change over five years is summarized in Figure 5.1.

How do all of those surplus countries play into this falling dollar picture? Remember, former Fed chairman Alan Greenspan observed

FIGURE 5.1 U.S. Dollar to Euro Exchange Rate, 2001–2007
(*Source:* OANDA.com.)

that in economics, the sum of all surpluses equals the sum of all deficits. So when a surplus country stops investing that surplus in U.S. dollars, its currency will increase against the dollar. This realization has profound implications. Not only does the dollar continue to fall against other currencies; as it does so, it accelerates the undesirability of pegging currencies to U.S. currency or investing in Treasury bonds and other debt. In other words, it becomes less and less viable for foreign investors and central banks to fund ever-growing U.S. debt.

This is not just a problem of U.S. consumer debt trends. We may be the addicts, but we have codependents and enablers around the world. Just as the U.S. consumer is addicted to spending excesses, foreign exporters have become addicted to selling goods to Americans. The problem is with sellers, as well as buyers. The governments in those other markets are as concerned about the U.S. dollar's fall as Americans are (or should be). Why? The fall of a dollar is the same thing as a rise in other currencies. So the competitiveness of the foreign export economy is damaged more and more as their own currencies increase in value. Just as a falling dollar hurts the buyer (Americans), a rising currency hurts the seller (foreign economies) in the same degree.

The United States is only one side of the problem. As the consumer, our dollars have tremendous influence throughout the world, if only because so many central banks (e.g., China's) have pegged their currency to the dollar—and at the same time many exporting nations are seeing their currencies going up in value, making it untenable to continue exporting at the same rates as in the past. So we have, through trillions of dollars of debt accumulation, created a de facto dollar standard in much of the world economy.

The debt is based, however, on a worldwide bubble economy, perhaps the biggest bubble in world history. The whole theory behind this comprehensive "bubblization" (a new word for you, referring to the combination of federal deficit, trade, mortgage, housing, dollar, and credit bubbles all working together) has grown out of the economic theories of the Fed. Although Mr. Greenspan was the chief culprit behind the theory that spending is good, more spending is better, and the most spending is best, we can't pin the whole thing on him. Like the U.S. consumer, he had enablers and codependents everywhere. His helpers include an array of bankers, corporate executives, and investors—all buying into the Greenspan version of the U.S. economy and how it just might work.

Now Mr. Bernanke, who happily puts himself out there as the leading economic forecaster and wise man, also contends that bubbles can't be recognized until they burst. That's like saying you can't tell that your house is on fire just because smoke is billowing from the windows; you have to wait until it bursts into flame. The truth is, bubbles are easily recognizable well in advance of bursting, but we cannot know *when* they will burst. The dollar bubble is going to burst, and that is inevitable. The effects on the economy of that burst are going to be serious. As long as investors, consumers, and business managers continue to base our financial decisions on assets of inflated and unrealistic value, we are denying this inevitable outcome. The more we depend on those inflated values, the more damage we will suffer when the bubble bursts.

In the case of Japan in the recent past, its pattern was somewhat different from the U.S pattern of today. Japan's deficit budget spending went into business investment, which in turn expands productivity and trade profits. Spending on business equipment and plans, commercial buildings, and other production-based infrastructure had a specific effect: When Japan's economy slowed down, it merely came to a halt and has remained chronically slow ever since. In comparison, U.S. deficit spending is overwhelmingly going into consumer spending with very little business investment or consumer savings to offset that trend. Thus, the U.S. trend in GDP is led by consumption and not by investment. So the use of deficit spending has everything to do with the consequences of deficits, and ultimately with the effect of a dollar crash. Unlike Japan's economy, which merely flattened out as a consequence of deficit spending, the U.S. economy is likely to see a more devastating change in the entire economic landscape—with the accompanying price inflation we have to expect as an outcome.

DENIAL AS A WAY OF LIFE

Unfortunately for the U.S. consumer, our Fed guy, Ben Bernanke, is not confronting the problem with any proposed solutions. Ignoring Warren Buffett's pragmatic abandonment of the U.S. dollar, Bernanke trumpets "productivity" and profit miracles in the U.S. economy. But real productivity has been flat and rising employment represents a shift out of manufacturing and into low-paying health care and retail jobs. No one can know for certain how much more of this kind of productivity the American economy can afford. It may depend on how long Mr. Bernanke has a job.

Like his old boss, Bernanke sees controlling inflation as the centerpiece of economic balance. But he contradicts this claim by pursuing policies that hurt the dollar. That's inflation. But even if we were to buy into the Fed's two-part economic theory, it still doesn't pan out.

This theory has a cause-and-effect ideal that goes something like this: Low inflation is an opportunity to print new money and to create ever-growing levels of consumer debt. Consumer debt leads to more consumer spending, and more spending is the same thing as prosperity.

Et voilà, you can now spend your way to wealth.

Well, a shot of whiskey is enjoyable and makes us feel good. But if we drink enough shots in one evening, it can kill us. How much credit growth can we afford? A *conservative* economic theory would limit credit growth so that it would never exceed savings. Putting this another way, we should never allow our liabilities to exceed our assets.

In the days prior to this current economic policy, it was almost universally recognized that it was a function of credit to transfer financial resources from savers to borrowers, as an orderly, predictable, and *controlled* aspect of leveraging assets. But the idea that credit could run unchecked above and beyond those assets was thought to be irresponsible—and it is. This is closely related to another piece of economic wisdom: that control over interest rates could speed up or slow down the economy. When spending accelerated, the Fed raised rates to slow things down. Today, the Fed keeps rates artificially low to encourage more spending. Why is the interest rate *artificially* low? There is a good reason. It is not based on purchasing coming from savings, nor from limitations on circulation of currency.

Clearly, the Fed is unwilling to recognize that there is only one real source of growth: a healthy and competitive environment involving the exchange of goods coupled with control over deficit spending. This is the flaw we saw in the Japanese economy a few years ago. Their failure to eliminate deficit spending ultimately held down the Japanese economy even when other economic attributes were strong.

If you listen to explanations from the Fed, you will conclude that the source of strength in the U.S. economy comes from three sources: First, we lead the world in information technology (IT); second, our free market entrepreneurial culture and the profit motive are unparalleled; third, the U.S. labor market has great flexibility.

All well and good, but the effects of these three features, or what we may collectively call our can-do attitude and know-how, are exaggerated by the Fed. When we look at actual performance by sector, we do not find a profit miracle, nor do we find expanding, competitive manufacturing. We see production jobs going overseas, the expansion of low-paying jobs, and the overall replacement of productive GDP growth with a different kind of GDP, that produced from spending rather than from profitability.

The United States is either giving away the capability to manufacture goods based on that technology or failing to compete in markets that are aggressively (and successfully) going after market share. We can look at a promising short-term trend in IT and call it an indicator of sorts, but in fact it was only a bubble. Another bubble. American businesses have not kept their lead, and, like other manufacturing sectors of our economy, they're losing to China and India—and other places around the world—almost as quickly as credit card debt is increasing. The onetime encouragement to "buy American" isn't possible any longer because so many of the products we purchase (like shoes, electronics, computers, and denim jeans, for example) are being manufactured in China, India, and other Asian and Central American countries. So no one can "buy American" any longer. Today, your only choice is to "spend American."

This drastic change in how the U.S. economy works may be accurately described as the replacement of real capitalism with show-business fictitious capitalism. We already know from looking at the numbers that the applauded "information age" didn't really create an American economic miracle. The overall effect was not a big splash, and it represented too small a share of GDP to count as a major trend. It was more like a short-term indicator that was contradicted by the larger economic trend—leading us toward spending. Between 2002 and 2007, for example, spending on information technology and hardware hovered around 2 percent of GDP, but no more: It is now less than 1 percent of GDP.

The most significant indicator in our economy was not productivity, but expansion of credit. Under Mr. Greenspan's term, U.S. credit
and debt added up to $8.505 trillion. That means it took $4.80 of new
debt to create one dollar of GDP. And now, with the burden of U.S.
credit and debt up to $9.149 trillion under his successor, Ben
Bernanke, it will take more than $5 to create one dollar of GDP. Every
additional dollar in credit *adds* a dollar to someone's debt—yours,
mine, the government's, or, realistically, the debt of future generations
of American taxpayers and consumers.

How did all this so-called disposable income develop? The housing
bubble. Homeowners were able to take out their equity and increase
their debt at ever-lower rates. This lopsided switch away from production and toward debt is at the heart of the declining dollar. Americans
no longer have gobs of equity to spend. And we're used to spending,
so then what happens?

In less than two years with Bernanke, our credit expanded from
$3 trillion to $3.3 trillion. But a funny thing happened in November
2007: Credit dropped by nearly 9 percent, back down to $3 trillion.
Maybe the rest of the world is sick and tired of our addiction to
cheap credit.

Globally, central banks dumped about $163 billion in U.S.
Treasuries. Not since Russia's 1998 default have U.S. Treasuries been
sold at such a pace. And these numbers are from September 2007—
before the Fed cut the overnight rate not once, but five times by
January 30, 2008.

PROFITS LOST

"History shows," wrote Jim Rogers in the foreword to our first
book, *Financial Reckoning Day* (John Wiley & Sons, 2003), "that people who save and invest grow and prosper, and the others deteriorate
and collapse." Business investment creates economic recoveries.
Without that investment, we have no right to expect a recovery. The
Fed and other monetary gurus claim that the low level of business
investment is to be blamed on excess inventories and low demand
overseas. But realistically, corporate America has gone through a
trend in the past two decades in which dwindling profits have led to

increased levels of mergers and acquisitions, but little change in the lagging profit picture. The belief, or the hope, that merging and internal cost cutting would solve profitability problems has been dashed. It hasn't worked.

Corporate America is coming to the point of having to face its own set of realities. Merging does not improve profits if the market itself is weak. Lacking real investment in plant and equipment, long-term growth is less likely today than before the merger mania and the growing trade deficit. Coupled with this is an expanding obligation for pension liabilities among large corporations. The problem of deceptive reporting isn't limited to the government. Corporations do the same thing.

Consider the following: Many corporations notoriously inflated their earnings reports—and not just Enron. Quite legitimately, and with the blessings of the accounting industry, companies exclude many big expense items from their operating statements and may include revenues that should be left out. Exclusions like employee stock option expenses can be huge. At the same time, including estimated earnings from future investments of pension plan assets is only an estimate, and cannot be called reliable. Standard & Poor's has devised a method for making adjustments to arrive at a company's *core earnings*. Those are the earnings from the primary business of the company, and anything reported should be recurring.

The adjustments aren't small. For example, in 2002, E.I. du Pont de Nemours (DuPont) reported earnings of more than $5 billion based on an audited statement and in compliance with all of the rules. But when adjustments were made to arrive at core earnings, the $5 billion profit was reduced to a $347 million *loss*; core earnings adjustments that year of nearly $5.5 billion had to be made. That is a big change. Other big negative adjustments had to be made that year for IBM ($5.7 billion reported profits versus $287 million in core earnings) and General Motors ($1.8 billion reported profits versus a $2.4 billion core loss). That year, the two largest core earnings adjustments were made by Citicorp ($13.7 billion in adjustments) and General Electric ($11.2 billion in adjustments).[4]

Here's where the question of realistic net worth comes into play: In accounting, any adjustment made in earnings has to have an offset somewhere. So when Citicorp overreports its earnings by $13.7 billion, that means it has also understated its liabilities by the same amount—a fact that should be very troubling to stockholders. One of the largest of the core earnings adjustments is unfunded pension plan liabilities. United Airlines, for example, announced in 2004 that it was going to stop funding pension contributions. After filing Chapter 11 bankruptcy in 2002, the United Airlines unfunded liability is an estimated $6.4 billion.[5]

When we hear that a corporation has not recorded employee stock option expenses of $1 billion, that also means the company's net worth is exaggerated by the same amount—and the book value of the company is exaggerated. So all of the numbers investors depend on are simply wrong. The escalating pension woes have been building up for years. A booming stock market a few years back added to corporate profits. But once the market retreated, those profits disappeared. In this situation, stock prices fall while ongoing pension liabilities rise. As employees retire, obligatory payments have to be made out of operating profits and—while few corporate types want to talk about this—those very pension obligations and depressed returns on invested assets may be a leading factor in the high number of corporate bankruptcies. Filing for bankruptcy often becomes the only way out when the corporations cannot afford to meet their pension obligations.

BORROWING WITH WILD ABANDON

Corporate management may be reined in, to some extent, by changes in federal law. The Sarbanes-Oxley Act changed the culture in some important ways. But until the accounting industry goes through some changes of its own, the corporate problem won't disappear. It appears so far that the disaster of Arthur Andersen has been viewed in the accounting industry as a public relations problem rather than what it really is: a deep, cultural failure within the business to protect the stockholders.

The parallels between corporate failures and government policy are alarming, if only because the Fed is not accountable to the Securities and Exchange Commission (SEC) or to stockholders in the same way that a corporate CEO and CFO are—and civil fines or imprisonment are out of the question. So as far as accountability is concerned, it looks like the borrowing and spending will continue—with yet more wild abandon.

The halfhearted debate over the twin deficits in trade and budget involve some big numbers, but the Fed is not concerned. In his penchant for understatement, Ben Bernanke is a lot like his old boss, Alan Greenspan. Read what he told the Charlotte, North Carolina, Chamber of Commerce in late November 2007, explaining why the Fed's monetary policy committee, the FOMC, decided to cut the short-term interest rate in October:

> Growth appeared likely to slow significantly in the fourth quarter from its rapid third-quarter rate and to remain sluggish in early 2008.[6]

Still, like Greenspan, Bernanke was upbeat, believing that growth will

> thereafter gradually return to a pace approaching its long-run trend as the drag from housing subsides and financial conditions improve.[7]

Although he admits that construction and home sales continued to be "weak," and that the unemployment rate had "drifted up" to 4.7 percent, he points to "solid" gains in the labor market in October. What gains? The 130,000 new jobs added to private-sector payrolls are mostly service and temp jobs. A rate of 4.7 percent is too close for comfort to 5 percent, the official mark when an economy is in recession.

Then he turns a bit more realistic, admitting the

> combination of higher gas prices, the weak housing market, tighter credit conditions, and declines in stock prices seem likely to create some headwinds for the consumer in the months ahead.[8]

Headwinds! That's a nice way of saying we're headed for stormy weather.

> The fresh wave of investor concern has contributed in recent weeks to a decline in equity values, a widening of risk spreads for many credit products (not only those related to housing), and increased

short-term funding pressures. These developments have resulted in a further tightening in financial conditions, which has the potential to impose additional restraint on activity in housing markets and in other credit-sensitive sectors.[9]

Analyze this for reality, taken from the burning pages of *The Daily Reckoning:*

> The credit bubble wouldn't have gotten so large were it not for the Fed. The Fed guarantees the solvency of the credit markets like Fannie Mae guarantees the solvency of the mortgage-backed security market. . . . Without Fannie Mae, mortgage-lending practices wouldn't have gotten crazy. . . . Without the Fed, the issuance of collateralized debt obligations (a type of asset-backed security that is as dubious as it sounds, funding portfolio investments with credit-risky, fixed-income assets) wouldn't have mushroomed. . . .

> "A rising tide lifts all fortunes," promises the saying—but not with this extreme form addiction to risky credit. Under terms of the agreement hammered out with lenders, only a fraction of an estimated 2.3 million subprime borrowers—an estimated 145,000–240,000 borrowers—will qualify for the freeze.

As borrowing increases as a percentage of GDP—up to more than 70 percent during the 1980s—savings rates fall and continue falling. By the end of the 1990s, borrowing had reached 90 percent of GDP, and reached 95 percent less than a decade later, in 2006. That's where the real damage is being done. And in the middle of the very same trend, nonfinancial business profits have been falling as well. The so-called U.S. expansion has been a nonexpansion. Corporate profits, which fell in the 1980s from 5.1 percent of GDP down to 3.7 percent, continue their downward spiral. By definition, a profitless expansion is not really an expansion at all. The bubble economy of the 1980s was the beginning of a worsening effect in real numbers that built throughout the 1990s and beyond.

CHAPTER 6

ATTENTION TO DEFICITS DISORDER

To contract new debts is not the way to pay old ones.

—George Washington

If the history of United States federal budgets—and the debts that grow out of them—tells us anything, it is this: The dollar's in it up to its eyeballs. Today's level of debt and continuing deficit spending is only the visible portion of that problem; beneath the surface we face an unavoidable day of reckoning for our great national pastime: spending money.

Since long before Lord Keynes opened his mouth in the 1930s, the attitude in Washington and among academics has been that we don't really have to ever repay debt. It can be carried indefinitely for future generations to worry about. Most today would claim that debt doesn't matter or even that it is a wise policy to spend more than you bring in. The mind boggles.

Early on in U.S. history, we Americans learned from our British ancestors that empires could be built on a foundation of debt—and continued indefinitely. In the early part of the eighteenth century, Sir Robert Walpole introduced an innovative system for financing Britain's colonial expansion and ever-growing military might. Government, Walpole demonstrated, is able to create a revenue stream by issuing bonds and other debt instruments. The interest is paid regularly, and eventually, upon maturity, the face value is paid off—*and for every maturing bond, a new one is issued*. This simple method for the expansion of revenue through debt was the venue by which Britain built its empire, from the 1720s through the next 100 years. Among those who observed this phenomenon of endless debt financing was the first secretary of the Treasury of the United States, Alexander Hamilton.

In the early days of the American nation, a host of fiscal problems faced Hamilton and the other Founding Fathers. The War for Independence left a large debt; there was no unified currency, and each state issued its own money; the currency itself was of dubious value; and inflation made it difficult to imagine how the young nation would even survive. Hamilton's view was that growth and expansion would be possible with the use of debt:

> Hamilton's rationale for a perpetual public debt included his belief that it would help keep up taxes and preserve the collection apparatus. He believed Americans inclined toward laziness and needed to be taxed to prod them to work harder.[1]

Not everyone agreed. In Thomas Jefferson's view,

> It was unjust and unrepublican for one generation of a nation to encumber the next with the obligation to discharge the debts of the first. After all, the following generation cannot have given their consent to decisions made by their fathers, nor will they have necessarily benefited from the deficit expenditures.[2]

During the nineteenth century, American debt did not grow substantially. When Jefferson began his first presidential term in 1801, the nation had an $83 million debt, mostly left over from the costs of the war. During his two terms, Jefferson reduced the debt to $37 million even after spending $15 million on the Louisiana Purchase.

In James Madison's term of office, the ill-fated War of 1812 ran the national debt up to $127 million by 1816. James Monroe and John Quincy Adams were both able to reduce the debt during their terms of office, and by 1829 the debt had fallen to $58 million. And then, during Andrew Jackson's presidency, the national debt was entirely paid off. For the first time in its history (and the last) the United States had no national debt.

Over the next decade, the country ran up $46 million in new debt and by 1848 the national debt had risen to $63 million. However, in all fairness, one advantage of this was that the Mexican War resulted in U.S. expansion all the way to the Pacific and the acquisition of the entire Southwest, including California. Under the Franklin Pierce administration, the debt was paid down to $28 million; but it never got that low again.

The Civil War exploded the national debt up to $2.8 *billion,* or 100 times higher than it had been in 1857. Debt in 1860 was $2 per capita; at the end of 1865, per capita debt was $75. The temporary tax measures in place during the war were repealed, and by the end of the nineteenth century the debt had been reduced to $1.2 billion, less than half of its 1865 level.[3]

Given the vast expansion of U.S. territory and the wars the country fought to create and then hold together the United States, this does not seem a large debt level. In fact, in its first 110 years of history, the United States had shown its ability to fund expansion while reducing debt over time. And this was accomplished without an income tax. In fact, in 1869 and again in 1895, the Supreme Court ruled federal income taxes unconstitutional.

The story was quite different in the twentieth century. By the end of World War I, the national debt had risen to $26 billion. Even though the debt level had been reduced over the next decade, the Great Depression caused further deficit spending, and FDR's New Deal tripled debt levels up to $72 billion.

World War II created yet higher debt levels. By 1945, the country owed $260 billion—small by today's standards but gargantuan in its time. One outgrowth of that war was a new one, the Cold War. Military spending took the national debt up to $930 billion by 1980, and under Ronald Reagan's administration it rose to nearly $2.7 trillion. In Bill Clinton's eight years, the debt more than doubled to $5.6 trillion. And by the end of 2007, the debt had passed $9 trillion—a nearly tenfold increase since 1980. The debt has doubled since George W. Bush took office in 2000. And by 2012, assuming current policy doesn't change (i.e., tax cuts are made permanent, the Alternative Minimum Tax is reformed, we are still funding the war in Iraq and building up the Department of Defense, and we don't extend 2007 emergency funding), our debt is expected to hit $12.3 trillion, according to a January 2007 estimate by the Congressional Budget Office (CBO). That's a 12-fold increase in the last quarter century. Quite descriptively, the CBO labeled its report "Building a Wall of Debt."

In other words, the national debt is growing exponentially. We may blame the War on Terror, the inheritance left by the Cold War, or the new international market and its competitive forces, or a combination of these realities. In any event, it is clear that the levels of debt keep setting new records, virtually on a month-to-month basis. The U.S. debt is growing at a rate of $1.4 billion a day, $1 million a minute; the most famous debt clock in the country, located on Times Square in New York City, will become obsolete once it hits the $10 trillion mark.

I love the following comments, issued in a joint October 2007 statement by Henry Paulson, the secretary of the U.S. Treasury, and Jim Nussle, the director of the administration's Office of Management and Budget. Paulson: "This year's budget results demonstrate the remarkable strength of the U.S. economy. This strength has translated into record-breaking revenues flowing into the U.S. Treasury and a continued decline in the federal budget deficit."

True, but: We still have a deficit.

Nussle: "Our short-term budget outlook is improving, but beyond the horizon is a huge budgetary challenge—the unsustainable growth in Social Security, Medicare, and Medicaid; . . . for the sake of our children and grandchildren, Congress should begin to take action to prevent this fiscal train wreck."

Figure 6.1 shows the level of the U.S. national debt from 1929 to the present.

In reviewing all of this history, we make a distinction between *debt levels* and *deficit spending*. Many people are confused about the differences, and some, even experts, use *debt* and *deficit* interchangeably.

A debt is the amount of money owed. A deficit is the shortfall in a current budget. For example, if we begin the year with a $6 trillion national debt, and during the year we spend $1 trillion more than we bring in, we are running a deficit of $1 trillion. By the end of the year, that deficit will have increased the debt to $7 trillion.

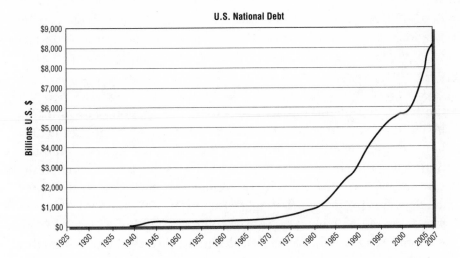

U.S. National Debt

FIGURE 6.1 U.S. National Debt, 1925–2007

(*Source:* U.S. Treasury.)

THE *REAL* DEFICIT SPENDING PROBLEM

Why does the government need to spend more than it takes in? After all, in most of the nineteenth century there were no income taxes (except during the Civil War). And the debts the nation incurred were paid down time and again. Even by 1900 the debt level was manageable. Not so today.

So what are the root causes of deficit spending and the resulting debt?

Debt itself has become institutionalized. Today, many people simply accept as a fact of life that the national debt is unimaginably high. The problem, though, is that we cannot continue the exponential expansion of debt without a catastrophic economic outcome. And it isn't just the stated trillions of dollars of official debt. If you add in the obligations of the U.S. government under Medicare and Social Security, the real overall debt is many times higher than the 2007 level of more than $9 trillion. The real debt is estimated as of 2007 at almost six times higher, about $53 trillion.[4] Other estimates are that such "mandatory spending programs . . . actually inflate the national debt by a factor of 10."[5]

How much is $53 trillion? It is difficult to imagine. A stack of $100 bills would be about five feet high to reach $1 million.

A $1 billion stack would be one mile high; and a $1 trillion stack would be 1,000 miles high. So $53 trillion would equal 53,000 miles of tightly stacked $100 bills, which would reach around the earth more than twice!

One problem with explaining the severity of U.S. debt levels is that the real scope of the problem is beyond imagination. This situation has been growing through the twentieth century and is going to come home to roost in our near future. Even during the Clinton administration, when the government boasted of "budget surpluses," there really was no surplus at all. Even if we confine the discussion to the stated debt, we realize that in the eight years from 1992 to 2000, the debt rose from $4.065 trillion to $5.674 trillion. The claimed surpluses, or what one scholar has called a "surplus hoax," were achieved through a little trickery:

> Imagine a corporation suffering losses and being deep in debt. In order to boost its stock prices and the bonuses of its officers, the corporation quietly borrows funds in the bond market and uses them not only to cover its losses but also to retire some corporate stock and thereby bid up its price. And imagine the management boasting of profits and surpluses. But that's what the Clinton administration has been doing with alacrity and brazenness. It suffers sizable budget deficits, increasing the national debt by hundreds of billions of dollars, but uses trust funds to meet expenditures and then boasts of surpluses, which excites the spending predilection of politicians in both parties.[6]

In the Clinton years, the administration churned obligations through short-term debt in the hope that interest rates would not increase. At the same time, the Congressional Budget Office estimated that federal spending for Social Security and Medicare would grow from 7.5 percent of gross domestic product (GDP) in 1999 up to 16.7 percent by 2040.[7] So the claim of budget surpluses was disingenuous not only insofar as it described the nominal national debt but also because it ignored the reality of ever-larger long-term obligations under government programs.

Clinton-era Treasury Secretary Robert Rubin's scheme was continued in a sense by Treasury head Paul O'Neill in the administration of George W. Bush. (This fiscal philosophy came to be known sarcastically as "Rubinomics.") By 2002, it was clear that neither party had any serious intention of respecting a debt ceiling. Although such a ceiling exists, it is constantly revised by Congress as the debt continues its upward acceleration unchecked.

The post-9/11 imperative to fight the War on Terror—coupled with a stated desire to jump-start the economy—led President Bush to present ever-higher budgets while insisting on tax cuts. Were these initiatives accompanied by a serious reduction in government itself, it would make sense; otherwise, we are left with ever-higher budgets in which spending is invariably higher than revenues. It has become clear that both parties and the entire federal government reside in their own economic cloud-cuckoo-land.[8]

Ironically, the Federal Reserve's attempts to stimulate the economy via ever-lower interest rates led to a huge expansion in credit, both among consumers and in government. So we ended up with a mortgage bubble in addition to the other economic bubbles brought about by debt-based economic expansion. As housing prices grew nationally by 5 to 7 percent per year, consumers continually refinanced to remove equity at lower and lower rates, further fueling the bubble.

The official position concerning economic expansion ignored the reality. Then-Fed Chairman Alan Greenspan repeatedly pointed to high levels of consumer spending as evidence of a strong economy. This ignored the basic economic principle that makes a distinction between productive and consumptive debt. An example of productive debt is investment in plant and machinery, which leads to higher and more competitive manufacturing—a type of activity that is falling in the United States, not rising. Economists recognize that productive debt leads to permanent and long-term economic growth. In contrast, consumptive debt—which is the modern basis for the economic "recovery" pointed to often by the Fed and the Bush administration— is spending to purchase material goods. The spending does not go into savings or investment; it merely involves buying more stuff. And the modern form of consumptive debt is based on growing levels of credit card and mortgage debt. The consumer-based credit problem mirrors the national debt (and longer-term national obligation) problem. It is growing.

In the past, conservative politicians stood for balanced budgets and fiscal responsibility—or at least that was the claim. But beginning with the Reagan years, the concept of lower taxes as a generator of higher revenues, what Bush senior once termed "voodoo economics," became the new rule. Reagan ran on the promise of smaller government, spending cuts, and balanced budgets. But in Reagan's very first year in office, in 1981, he asked Congress to increase the statutory debt limit above $1 trillion. Argued for as a one-time measure needed to bring the economic house into line, this departure opened up a new era; and now, a quarter century later, we find ourselves at nine times the $1 trillion "magic number" of the pre-Reagan debt ceiling. The inane argument offered up by Professor Abba Lerner in the 1930s that there is nothing wrong with a national debt because "we owe it to ourselves"[9] demonstrates the twisted thinking used to justify current policies. It is the same thing as saying it is all right as consumers to pile on mortgage debt on our homes because "we owe it to ourselves" in the sense that it is our equity. Astute homeowners would not accept such a vacuous argument; and yet it is offered with a straight face by some economists concerning the national debt.

Another justification is often put forth that the U.S. "net worth" justifies ever-higher debt levels. In other words, as long as our assets are higher than our liabilities, a large national debt is no problem. Vast land holdings via national parks and preserves, government buildings, and other valuable assets, for example, are cited as examples that we have nothing to worry about. However, this argument fails on the merits. In corporate balance sheets, one justification for growing debt would be that it enables the expansion of markets and capital assets. But let us not forget that *the federal government produces nothing*. The debt may go partially for necessities or entitlements that large segments of the population want to continue, but the debt itself is *not* an example of productive debt. So the arguments that it's okay because (1) we owe it to ourselves or (2) our assets are greater than our liabilities are both false justifications for a problem that, ultimately, may define the collapse of the entire U.S. economy.

In fact, we don't "owe it to ourselves." The portion of the national debt held by foreign central banks grows month after month, and in the near future a majority of the stated debt will be held overseas. At the end of 2006, the amount of our debt held by foreigners had increased by $463.9 billion during the year, to $2.7 trillion. That's 46 percent of the national debt at the time—up from 44 percent in 2005. Two percentage points in a year is a very big deal.

Economists enjoy comparing government debt to entrepreneurial debt. The highly leveraged business owner Donald Trump has suffered financial reversals and even the bankruptcy of his casino empire; but at least he provides jobs, construction activity, and commerce for thousands of people. His debt, while leveraged, is an example of productive debt. But it makes the point that in spite of the long-standing belief that people in debt are habitually poor and creditors are habitually rich, it often is the other way around. In fact, in business the more successful entrepreneurs are often also the most in debt (but *productive* debt). This has no comparison to government debt, which—again, it may be classified as necessary or even contractual with the people receiving entitlements—is *not* a form of productive debt. As long as Congress has the attitude that higher revenues (even if artificial) open the door to higher spending levels, this economic promiscuity is not likely to end, at least not until the end is imposed upon Congress, and upon the people.

Government spending is not productive for two reasons. As explained earlier, government produces nothing in the form of investment or capital assets. But in addition, it generates no revenues. It finances its own growth and expansion in three ways. First is tax revenue, or taking of money from people, corporations, and imports. Second is inflation, a system under which debt literally loses value and can be repaid with depreciated dollars. Third is debt itself, an expansion of the system that has no end until an end is imposed upon government. In the nineteenth century, a series of presidents took debt seriously and, other than in periods of war, diligently paid down the national debt. It may be coincidental, but that all changed at about the same time that the federal income tax was imposed. After repeated decisions by the U.S. Supreme Court that the federal tax was unconstitutional, the Court finally accepted the tax in 1913. Since then, deficit spending has become the rule and balanced budgets the exception. The concept of actually paying down the debt is an oddity. The even more distant idea of eliminating the federal debt is viewed as unrealistic, even un-American. But we should recall the warning provided 250 years ago by Adam Smith:

It is the highest impertinence and presumption . . . in kings and ministers to pretend to watch over the economy of private people, and to restrain their expense.[10]

The chosen path of the United States, in spite of Smith's wise warning, was to come to view the national debt as a "national blessing."[11] Well, an unbridled spending program may indeed be viewed as a national blessing by those in Congress, and among economists who justify debt levels by classifying the debt as productive debt. But any honest study of how and where government spending occurs would have to conclude that the undisciplined growth of the debt is anything but productive.

THE COST OF OUR "NATIONAL BLESSING"

Loads of people in government—notably in the Bush administration and among the leaders of the Federal Reserve—believe, perhaps sincerely, that deficit spending is a positive force, that it works to improve the economy, and that it has no lasting negative consequences. Congress appears either to agree with this point of view or to go along with it in the interest of spending ever higher levels of public money. Even though expressed as a joke, we should view Congress in light of a new congressman's comment,

> I've had a tough time learning how to act like a congressman. Today I accidentally spent some of my own money.[12]

One of the most destructive facts—and one obstructing any reform of the problem—is that those in Congress do *not* think about public money as real money. There exists an intentional self-imposed disconnect between what Congress spends and who pays for it.

Complicating the dialogue is the never-ending class warfare surrounding government spending and tax policy itself. Republicans claim that tax cuts stimulate growth and improve the jobs situation, thus improving the economy overall. Democrats criticize the "huge tax cuts for the rich" as a burden on less fortunate Americans. Both arguments are flawed in some degree, but the appeal is made to distinct voting blocs. Class warfare based on envy and resentment does nothing to improve the understanding of the problem among the people; in fact, arguments made with a political bias only close the door to any meaningful education or discussion of the problem—ever-higher debt

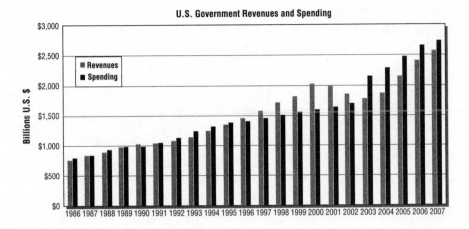

FIGURE 6.2   U.S. Government Revenues and Spending, 1986–2007
(*Source:* Congressional Budget Office.)

(of both the public and the government), trade deficits, and numerous economic bubbles.

In the final analysis, it does not matter whether we raise or lower taxes if spending outpaces revenue. Higher taxes affect consumers; but higher government spending that consistently outpaces its own tax revenues does greater damage in the long term. Consider the comparison between revenue and outlays for the 22 years from 1986 to 2007 in Figure 6.2.

We should not overlook the important differences between government deficits and individual deficits. While these differences may be obvious to many, one Congressional report did a good job of comparing the two, in respect not only to their attributes but also to the economic consequences and ramifications involved. Pointing out that an individual is able to offset deficits by working harder, spending less, or applying for a temporary loan, the report notes:

> In contrast, government revenue comes mainly from taxes, which are compulsory. When government increases its revenue by increasing its tax collections, there is no presumption that people will be better off. They may not want to give more of their income to the government. Therefore, closing a budget deficit by raising more revenue does not necessarily make the economy grow; it can discourage growth by making leisure time and other untaxed activity relatively more

attractive. Raising tax rates, or keeping them higher than they need be, increases what economists call the "deadweight loss" or "excess burden" of taxation—income that is not transferred from taxpayers to government, but is simply lost because excessive taxation reduces economic growth by inducing people to behave less productively.[13]

This observation is true, but it refers to only part of the problem. History has demonstrated that tax policy does *not* help eliminate deficits. Increased taxes have *not* closed budget deficits, but have only inspired Congress to spend more; and reductions in the tax rate have one of two outcomes, depending on which side you believe: Either these lower taxes only add to the deficit, or the resulting "trickle-down" revenues—again—result in higher annual budgets and the resulting higher deficits.

A HISTORY OF DEFICIT SPENDING

A recurring argument in all of this debate over taxes and the national debt is that deficit spending actually helps the economy through stimulus. In fact, government has come to view its role in the economy as a driving force that can and should take steps to fix recessions or to curb inflation. In times of recession, the proposal to increase government spending is invariably argued as a method for fixing the problem.[14]

This argument defies logic. Since government produces nothing, there is no logical way that increased spending would have any positive effect on the economy. Were the argument made to increase investment in manufacturing plant and equipment, provide incentives to higher savings, or actually reduce government deficit spending, it might make sense. But claiming that higher spending on the part of government would fix an economic recession is like claiming that the best way to put out a fire is to pour gasoline on a burning house.

There are situations in which deficit spending has a positive impact on the economy, but such instances are limited, to say the least. When such spending reallocates resources from less productive use and into more productive use, it is conceivable that deficit spending would improve a weak economy. But as a general observation, government spending has the opposite effect, reallocating resources from more productive use and into *less* productive use.[15]

The problem with using taxing policy in an attempt to control the economy has historically been ineffective. This may be true in part because tax policy has so often been used to reward or punish, to feed into the class warfare and resentment we see in different voting groups. Tax policy has done more to widen the gap between classes than any other force in U.S. history. The problem goes beyond the arrogance to believe that the economy can be tinkered with, as though a simple adjustment of the tax thermostat is all it takes to fix the problem.

Tax policy is far more complex and the consequences of changes in policy invariably belie even the best of intentions. This inevitability was explained more than 150 years ago by Senator John C. Calhoun, who stated:

> On all articles on which duties can be imposed, there is a point in the rate of duties which may be called the maximum point of revenue—that is, a point at which the greatest amount of revenue would be raised. If it be elevated above that, the importation of the article would fall off more rapidly than the duty would be raised; and, if depressed below it, the reverse effect would follow: that is, the duty would decrease more rapidly than the importation would increase.[16]

Although Calhoun was arguing about a tariff bill, the same point applies to the income taxes; the difficulty is in identifying the "maximum point of revenue." That varies depending on the political party in power, the desired voting bloc to which the speaker is appealing, and the economic perception in play. It appears evident that the point resides somewhere around a 20 percent effective tax rate. Above that level, individual behavior erodes economic performance and, thus, revenues.[17]

The point is, the government can't control the economy through tax policy—a lesson the government has yet to learn.

The recent economic history of the United States has been based on the premise that government initiatives can (and should) affect and even alter the course of the economy. Looking back, we see a clear distinction between the eras in U.S. history. From 1789 through

1912, government appeared to understand that the economy operated independently from government. In fact, as national debts were accumulated (as during the Revolutionary War, the War of 1812, and the Civil War), subsequent administrations paid those debts down. The presidents during those first 125 years or so took their responsibilities seriously, and recognized the real nature of the national debt.

Government does hold the power to finance its various programs, and even wars, through building up national debt. But that debt—at least during the first 125 years of U.S. history—was *not* viewed as a permanent fixture in the U.S. economy. Rather, the view appears to have been that debts accumulated in one period must be reduced or paid off in another.

From 1913 forward, we entered a different phase. Beginning with the three major changes that occurred that year (passage of the Federal Reserve Act, elimination of state legislature election of senators, and creation of the federal income tax), the whole view toward the economy and the government's role changed once and for all. Monetary policy was no longer viewed as an adjunct of government's economic role; it became a primary tool in the control over the pace and direction of the economy itself. Government became the economic god in the twentieth century, and monetary and tax policy was available to reward allies and to punish enemies.

With this new direction—used quite specifically by Presidents Wilson, Roosevelt, Nixon, and Clinton, for example—the line between economic policy and political incentive grew ever less distinct. Today, we see no line whatsoever. Economic and monetary policies are debated along party lines for the most part, with both sides pushed farther apart as the political debate heats up and as the next election cycle approaches.

The fallout from this nearly 100 years of monetary adventurism has no end in sight. We've lived with an income tax for nearly 100 years, but our national debt is higher than ever; in fact, it is higher than anyone could have imagined in 1913. Is there a connection? Clearly, there is. The nature of government is to spend more than it receives, and, as the income tax has become an institution in the United States, government spending has consistently outpaced revenues. Prior to 1913, debts came and went, but importantly, they went. Presidents and Congress did not overspend because the revenues simply were not available, so the lack of an income tax made it impossible to accelerate the debt problem.

Today, when the gold standard is but a distant memory, it has become possible for the United States and the Federal Reserve to authorize reduced interest rates and increased deficit spending.

If we look back to the decisions made during the Nixon administration, two forces were at work. First was inflation, a chronic problem Nixon tried to fix with wage and price controls and import tariffs. Second was the overprinting of money that led to the risk of a run on gold—the so-called international margin call. Nixon's solution was simply to remove the United States from the gold standard and allow unending printing of money.

It is the printing of unpegged fiat money that led to yet more inflation. In more recent years, government and the Federal Reserve have figured out how to make it look as though no inflation is taking place. Low interest rates equal no inflation, right? According to the Federal Reserve, low rates are good for the economy. But by definition, inflation means a loss of spending power. That can be viewed as one of two outcomes: higher prices or less purchasing power for our dollars.

As we measure inflation, it is elusive. The consumer price index (CPI) includes many components—food, durable goods, housing, fuel, and more. Often, as one price sector rises, another falls. On balance, we have a published rate of inflation that is supposed to explain how our dollar buys more or less. A shortfall between wages and prices means a loss of spending power, under traditional definitions. But if we measure the dollar against the euro, we get a more realistic view of inflation. In fact, as more and more fiat money is printed, we continue to lose spending power, which is most accurately measured against other currencies.

Among the changes that followed Nixon's 1971 decision was a change in the way that government debt was financed. Deficit finance bonds are sold through the financial markets to private investors. Of course, "private investors" does not limit the market to mutual funds or individuals in the United States; overseas central banks are included as well. The bond market exploded as a result of this change. In 1970, less than $1 trillion in bonds were issued. By 2006, the volume grew to $45 trillion.[18]

The change has, effectively, made price inflation invisible in the U.S. landscape. Author Peter Warburton has summarized this problem:

> Periodic bouts of price inflation, the tell-tale signs of a long-standing debt addiction, have all but vanished. The central banks, as financial physicians, seem to have effected a cure. . . . Few have bothered to ask how the central banks have accomplished this feat, one which has proven elusive for more than 20 years. As long as inflation is absent, who really cares exactly what the central banks have been up to?[19]

It is naive to believe—or to act upon the assumption—that prices of goods will naturally or automatically change based on the supply of money in circulation. (In other words, today's goods cost $1 to produce and sell for $2 retail; so if currency in circulation increases, costs rise to $2 and the retail price goes up to $4.) In fact, this is not how inflation works. Even so, it would seem that the U.S. government and the Federal Reserve believe this to be the case. A weak dollar diminishes the economic impact of the national debt and trade surplus, so that is a good thing, is it not?

Even if we were to accept the flawed premise dictating that changes in the money supply can, by association, affect prices, it makes no sense that this presumption also makes it acceptable to grow trade deficits and the national debt to higher and higher levels. The belief requires us to accept another premise: that we can solve all economic problems and shortfalls by continuing to print more and more money.

Many economists have had the uncomfortable suspicion for some time now that the U.S. government is playing the game of interest rate arbitrage, a practice begun under the Clinton administration and a cornerstone of Rubinomics. This "carry trade" involves selling low-yielding, short-term Treasury bills and using the money to buy much higher-yielding, longer-term notes and bonds. In other words, the concept involves using U.S. debt to profit from the differences between the debt tiers. Even if this worked, it would not justify the endless printing of more currency.

So the two practices—operating on the assumption that currency in circulation controls prices, and promoting interest rate arbitrage—are part of U.S. economic policy. The Achilles' heel of such a plan (even if we accept the underlying premises of each side) is that as long as the United States continues to accumulate annual deficits (as well as trade surpluses and other economic bubbles), the U.S. dollar will continue to weaken. This real inflation may not have an immediate impact on consumer prices across the board, but its ramifications are certainly felt in both equity and debt investment markets. Lower yields reflect not only historically low interest rates, but a growing recognition in the markets that the dollar's purchasing power is falling. In a very real sense, a decline in investment values reflects the inflationary spiral. Our modern variety of inflation is seen not in prices and wages directly as in the Nixon years, but in stock and bond prices.

During the ill-fated 1972 campaign of George McGovern— double-digit points behind Nixon in the weeks before election day— the candidate made an attempt to swing the mood in his favor. He promised $1,000 to every American man, woman, and child. But failing to articulate how he would pay for this, how much it would cost, or what it was meant to accomplish, the idea only increased Nixon's lead. Voters instinctively recognized that the proposal was a lame one. Were we to increase everyone's bank account by $1,000, we would inevitably see inflation as an offset, either in higher prices or in reduced purchasing power of the dollar. The electorate didn't buy McGovern's plan then, but, ironically, a similar approach to the economy permeates government and Federal Reserve policy today. The unlimited printing of fiat money enabled us to think that we would expand and grow forever, in a credit and debt bubble without end.

"Household net worth may not continue to rise relative to income," Alan Greenspan admitted early in 2005, "and some reversal in that ratio is not out of the question. If that were to occur, households would probably perceive the need to save more out of current income; the personal savings rate would accordingly rise, and consumer spending would slow."[20]

Was he ever wrong. The exact opposite happened: Personal savings fell below zero, while consumer spending increased. The impact took the air out of the subprime mortgage and credit bubbles.

In the third quarter of 2007, the Mortgage Bankers Association reported that the number of Americans who fell behind on their mortgage payments rose to a 20-year high. An incredible 5.59 percent of all home loans in the United States were at least 30 days late on one or more monthly payments—the worst delinquency rate since 1986—and one in every five subprime adjustable-rate mortgages suffered a late payment.

Does the Fed have a solution? Sure—but it's only for a chosen few: about 145,000 to 240,000 borrowers who began facing rate resets beginning in the third quarter of 2007. Bernanke estimated that 450,000 borrowers will face the music every month, so we're talking 2.3 million by the end of 2008. Meanwhile, the ratings agencies keep lowering the boom on the mortgage-backed assets or securities that funded these mortgages. The count is now somewhere in the neighborhood of a thousand bonds and securities that have been downgraded—and we're not done yet.

Like Mr. Greenspan, Mr. Bernanke also bemoans the possibility of slower production and profits among American companies as though that trend were separate from the Fed's monetary policies. In November 2007, the Institute for Supply Management (ISM) reported that U.S. manufacturing grew at its slowest pace in 10 months, 50.8 (once that measure falls to 50, ISM considers the sector to be in "contraction"). The service sector—where ISM considers 80 percent of the economy to lie, by the way—didn't do well, either: The index fell to 54.1 from October's 55.8, making November the worst month since March. (Until, that is, January of 2008, when it fell to 41.) In fact, a corporate trend toward soft or falling profits accompanied a business trend—starting in the 1980s—away from investment in tangible assets and more toward speculation. We know now that much of the reportedly spectacular corporate growth of the 1990s was the result not of profitable growth, but of accounting manipulation.

A PERVERSE INCENTIVE

The ill-conceived concept that executive compensation should be based on reported profits only invited the kind of abuses everyone saw in corporations like Enron and Tyco, and even among accounting firms like Arthur Andersen. Was this a symptom of the mood, both corporate and economic? Was the phony growth created out of pure greed, or was it only a symptom of a larger problem?

These are troubling questions. Without any doubt, the corporate deceptions that took place throughout the 1990s created a phony recovery that only delayed facing the truth. And a lot of greed was involved. But on a larger scale, this corporate deception went hand in hand with the Fed policies Mr. Greenspan promoted throughout his tenure. The 1990s asset bubble had a huge impact on the economy of the time, and consumers are now paying the price. We did not have a strong economy during that period, but government and corporate America went to great pains to make it look as though we did.

To appreciate the impact of this fake economic strength, we have to consider four distinct features: changes in the trend moving away from investment and toward consumption, profitability, the trade balance, and growth of debt.

DEBT ON STEROIDS

One day we hear about consumer debt, and on another we're told that savings rates are falling. But most people don't know how this affects them *or* the purchasing power of their dollar. With ever-expanding consumption, savings rates are down below zero of disposable income. And for all the money Americans accumulate on credit cards and higher mortgage debt, the federal government budget deficit is expanding at an even greater rate.

The warnings given out in the 1990s pale in comparison to the bigger bubbles we face now. Even though the housing bubble has begun to burst, it's still not over. But a related, less obvious change is taking place as well. A large portion of newly created credit flows into the financial markets—you know, *lenders* who, through mortgages, credit cards, and lines of credit, collect interest on this rising consumer debt. On one side, as the debt rises, so do the revenues from interest within those financial markets. On the other, when debts default, revenues evaporate, as we've seen from massive writedowns being taken by banks in the wake of the subprime mortgage mess.

Our basic economics instructor would remind us that recovery requires business confidence in the economy, and that confidence takes the form of investment in plant, equipment, and inventory. This is the key to increasing American standards of living and to sustained productivity (translation: higher-wage jobs, competitive industry, reduction of the trade deficit).

How do we move from today's poor economic situation characterized by a pillaged business infrastructure and return to the days of American dominance over world manufacturing? American corporations do not generally accumulate productive capital today; they, like the consumer, acquire debt to hold their ratios steady. Look at Motorola, for example. This company was a leader in affordable electronics for many years, before market share began to slip and move overseas. The solution? Motorola increased its long-term debt. This enabled the company to keep a strong working capital ratio (because current cash balances rose as long-term debt obligations were taken on), meaning that *current* assets and liabilities maintained the equilibrium of more profitable days. But in fact, the stockholders are stuck with long-term obligations to pay interest on those debt levels, in an environment where the company's revenues and profits are falling. In spite of what our Fed chairman says, increasing debt is *not* productivity. It is a disastrous policy.

Table 6.1 shows the numbers for the period from 1999 through 2006 for Motorola. In the same time span, sales dwindled. So did profits. The company lost money every year—even while its working capital ratio remained steady. This was a corporate version of the way the government runs its own monetary show. The theme here: Debt

TABLE 6.1 Motorola Long-Term Stockholders' Total Debt (in $millions)

Year	Debt	Equity	Capitalization	Ratio
1999	$3,089	$18,693	$21,782	14.2%
2000	4,293	18,612	22,905	18.7
2001	8,372	13,691	22,063	37.9
2002	7,189	11,239	18,428	39.0
2003	6,675	12,689	19,364	34.5
2004	4,578	13,331	17,909	34.3
2005	3,806	16,673	20,479	22.8
2006	2,704	17,142	19,846	13.6

Source: Motorola annual reports, at www.motorola.com.

is good, and more debt is fine. The problem, however, is that as equity capitalization is replaced by long-term debt, the ability of the company to compete fails. From a corporate point of view, there is less profit available for dividends and working capital as more and more goes to debt repayment and interest. On the government level, our "stock" is the value of our dollar. And as we consumers and our government spend more and more, as our businesses also use debt to finance operations, and as the trade and budget deficits run out of control, our "stock" (the purchasing power of the dollar) will become ever weaker.

If corporations depend too heavily on debt capitalization at the expense of equity, it eventually spells doom for them. Over the past few years, Motorola returned to profitability by putting a stop to its debt and taking a more realistic approach to its cash flow and profitability budgeting. The Fed could learn a lot from this lesson in basic economics.

Instead, what they term "wealth creation" is nothing more than that infamous series of bubbles. Clearly, growth in housing values leading to refinancing, higher transactions, and inflation in housing values is not wealth creation; it is credit expansion. If we spend more in consumption than in production, we do not get richer; we get poorer. The same is true for a nation.

Rising stock values or housing values add to equity and immediate net worth. As an individual, if your home doubles in value, then your capital is worth twice as much. But remember, this wealth creation is real in a sense because you invested money in real estate. If the same profitability occurred in the stock market, it would be because you invested money in stocks.

The equivalent of this type of growth for a nation involves investment in economic expansion—business inventories, plant, and equipment; competitive trade imports and exports; and sound monetary policies. But when we take another look at consumer profitability, what are we doing with our profits? If we refinance the mortgage on appreciated property and then spend the proceeds, we have *spent* our profits. If we had instead invested those profits in more real estate, in stocks or mutual funds, or in other equity positions, it would be different. The nation has, in a similar manner, allowed and even encouraged wealth destruction through its interest rate policies and by failing to provide businesses with incentives. The only incentive the government appears to offer—and this is its broadly based economic policy—is to keep interest rates low so that everyone can borrow. So business owners, consumers, and even students can afford more debt because of government monetary policy. All money has become easy, and the now ancient concept of "tight money" is a problem that the Fed has solved—by printing more money.

There is a tendency among economists—including the Fed chairman—to explain away current conditions without really exploring the underlying causes. For example, we are told that the cause of the sharp decline in business investment is prior overinvestment and excess capacity. Let's examine these two causes.

Prior overinvestment implies that business has put too much capital into manufacturing plant and equipment. But wait a minute. The statistics show that for at least a decade, manufacturing has been flat. There has not been any growth. So *if* it were true that business has invested too much, why hasn't it worked? The established economic wisdom tells us that when business invests in its own capital resources, that creates an improved—and more productive—environment. There is no statistical or actual evidence of overinvestment.

Excess capacity means, when you boil it down, that manufacturers have made too much stuff. So it would be piling up in warehouses, in containers, and on docks waiting for customers to place orders. Is that happening? Are business inventories too high? Let's take a look at the actual numbers:

At the end of January 2005, all manufacturers' inventory had increased 1.3 percent in one month. The prior month (December) saw an increase of 0.1 percent, and November's was 1.0 percent. These are not large changes. But an even more revealing statistical trend is seen in the published inventory-to-sales ratio for all U.S. manufacturers. See Figure 6.3.

The chart shows that manufacturing trends have been very consistent. If manufacturers were producing more than they could sell, we would see that, but that simply isn't the case. In fact, the ratio of inventory to sales has been *falling* steadily through the period, not rising.

The *real* case of falling business investment is consumer spending, combined with the trade gap. We're going further into debt and buying stuff from overseas rather than from domestic manufacturers—and the

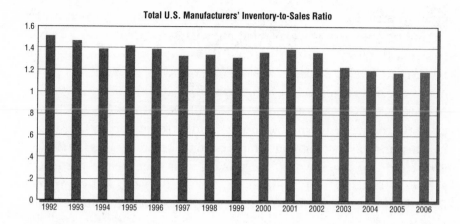

FIGURE 6.3 U.S. Manufacturers' Inventory-to-Sales Ratio, 1992–2006
(*Source:* U.S. Census Bureau.)

numbers prove it. We have ever-falling portions of total GDP going into net investment in manufacturing plants and equipment, and, as domestic demand for homemade products falls, the domestic manufacturing picture—as indicated by the inventory data—continues to get worse. Our manufacturers are not producing too much. They're producing less, in fact, because American goods are not competing with the goods made elsewhere.

Let's take another look at the nonfinancial sector—including the total of manufacturing, retail, and all other industries outside of investing, banking, insurance, mortgage brokerage, and other broadly defined financial corporations. We have to break out the nonfinancial and financial if we want to see what is really going on.

Fixed capital investment in the nonfinancial sector (that includes plants and equipment and other *capital* assets) represented 34.2 percent of real GDP[21] between 1997 and 2000. This is the highest ratio in U.S. history. Now if we look at a comparison between capital investment and unadjusted GDP, the outcome is only 7.3 percent of GDP during the same years. Why the big difference?

The types of spending affect the numbers, and so does the relative value of the dollar. And the method of reporting is inaccurate as well. The economists reported "spending" on computers in 2004 at $246.7 billion. But real spending was only $93.3 billion because the official statistics included the cost of computers produced and not the computers sold. As we explained in Chapter 2, the BEA stopped reporting the lower number because they said it was misleading. But the bottom line? Because higher numbers are reported, it looks like there's a recovery in place, when there isn't.

This deceptive report is similar to one of the corporate practices that got some companies in trouble in the late 1990s through 2001. Among the questionable accounting practices was booking sales based on production—in other words, recognizing sales even before the orders had been placed. This is without any doubt a no-no, and companies were required to restate their earnings when they were caught. It would be as though you went to the bank to get a loan, and reported this year's income at three times what you'll actually receive. Your justification: you expect to be employed for the next three years, so you're counting the future income this year. Your banker would never accept that kind of accounting. So why does our government get away with it?

We are left with a statistical muddle in Commerce Department reports. The reality, though, if we cut through the numbers, is that U.S. manufacturers have not overinvested in capital assets, nor have they produced excess inventory. In fact, one sign of our failing competitiveness is the change in net investment—and in the value of capital stock—since the 1980s. Both indicators have been representing increasingly lower portions of GDP throughout the period.

Economic forecasts—like the weather variety—are entertaining, surely, but they are wrong as often as they are right. The interpretation of the numbers and explanations about why conditions exist are suspect. It makes you wonder: Do economists and policy wonks really know what they're talking about? Like any academic exercise, their opinions are largely theoretical.

The only way to prevent a big correction in stocks and bonds, continuing loss of purchasing power, and losses in competitiveness in world markets is to correct the imbalances and dislocations the numbers point to. But the Feds are not taking any action. Their policy, "Inflate, inflate," only aggravates the problem. Even so, the strategy remains official U.S. monetary policy.

We've explained how consumer spending and lagging business competitiveness decimate our economy. But these issues have to be viewed in conjunction with the chronic gap between policy and reality in the enormous trade deficit and external current account deficit, which deserves another look now in light of the business trends we can demonstrate through statistics (versus what the official explanation concludes). Beginning in 1960 we had a trade *surplus*. That lasted through to 1977, when our downward spiral began and the gap has grown ever since.

As deficits became the rule, the annual volume of trade also grew. The problem is a package deal: out-of-control consumer spending, damaging monetary policies, expanding trade gaps, federal budget deficits, lagging competitiveness in American businesses, and aggressive manufacturing growth in Asia. The big question among world economists is, can the current account deficit in the United States be sustained? The consensus is that it cannot.

The current account deficit is different from the trade deficit. It adjusts for the value of foreign investment on both sides of the trade picture.

We have seen the trade gap trend. Now let's review the current account deficit. (See Figure 6.4.) To the casual observer or to one who simply watches the trade deficit, the problem has become severe enough. But when we also consider the change in investment—in other words, the current account deficit—the picture looks far worse. In fact, few people outside as well as within the government seem to realize

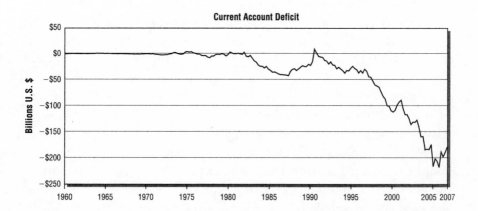

FIGURE 6.4 Current Account Deficit, 1960–2007

(*Source:* Bureau of Economic Analysis.)

that the imbalances in these international economic trends represent the most dangerous economic problem for the United States since 1929.

Domestic monetary policy has its roots in many causes, including trade and current account deficits, increased borrowing and spending, loss of competitive edge, and the removal of the U.S. dollar from the gold standard. Within five years of the decision to go off the gold standard in 1971, the trade surplus had turned into a deficit, and within a decade following that shift, the current account balance plummeted downward as well.

All of this relates directly to the loss of purchasing power. In the past, U.S. economic strength grew from dominance in the world manufacturing markets, and the dollar was king. But once we gave up that lead, it was inevitable that the dollar would fall. A major beneficiary, European currency, was inevitable.

The strong euro is a direct result of changes in international trade and manufacturing and in expectations about future investment rates of return. A prevailing perception among U.S. economists has been that Europe's economy has been purely export-driven, but this has proven to be wrong. The falling U.S. dollar has not harmed European exporting by creating cheaper imports in the United States. An international perception that the U.S. consumer has an insatiable appetite for goods has held up import prices. That perception has been accurate.

In fact, prolonged softness in U.S. productivity and record-low interest rates are beginning to make the United States unattractive for foreign investors. This will only accelerate the dollar's decline and, as a consequence, create big losses in the domestic markets.

The United States failed to take quick steps to stop the trade gap from worsening in the late 1970s. Once the surplus disappeared and deficits began to increase, it was time for immediate action. But it seems that at the time no one understood the severity of the problem or how bad it was going to get. Certainly, no one seemed to understand the impact on the dollar's long-term purchasing power.

We cannot avoid a logical cause and effect between the dollar and the domestic investment markets. Just as a strong dollar strengthens the market, it stands to reason that by the same argument a weak dollar also weakens the markets.

The euro's strength has not resulted from any Europe-specific economic changes. The euro's rise could be called a bull run without any bulls. Rather, adverse economic and financial trends are doing severe damage to the dollar and—all currencies being relative—as the dollar falls the value of the euro rises.

THE YING AND THE YANG (BUT NOT THE YEN AND THE YUAN)

The current account deficit is the most immediate problem affecting the dynamic value changes between the two currencies, and that discussion begins with an analysis of the trend in the trade deficit. The question that should be asked is:

> At current exchange rates, the strength of the U.S. economy, combined with slow growth in demand in many other parts of the world, will lead to further widening of the U.S. trade deficit. How long can the trade deficit continue on that trajectory without disrupting the U.S. economy or the world economy?[22]

That's exactly the concern among European and Asian economists today. It's not just the problem we face now, but the prospect of those conditions continuing on into the future and getting worse—not to mention the difficulties involved with any real fix.

The changes needed include adjustments in exchange rates; a slowdown in U.S. growth, notably in consumer spending; improvement in demand in foreign countries for U.S. goods (requiring big changes in the competitive nature of U.S. manufacturing); and through these changes, a gradual reduction of the trade deficit—perhaps with visions of future trade balances or, perhaps, a trade surplus.

Are these changes really possible? As recently as 1998, the current account deficit was at 2.3 percent of GDP. By the middle of 2004 it had doubled to 5 percent, and in 2006 it went higher still, to 6 percent. That is a lot of deterioration in only eight years, and signs point to ever-widening future current account deficits. The adjustment can be brought about through changed policies, or worldwide economic changes will force the adjustment. One big concern is the disparity in exchange rates, not so much because as one currency rises another falls, but more because of the structure in U.S. assets versus debts. More than one-half of U.S. foreign assets are denominated in foreign currencies, while the vast majority (88 percent) of our liabilities are dollar-denominated. This disparity in currencies could have unintended consequences based on the movement in currency values of the dollar as well as other currencies.

The first impulse among U.S. policy makers often is to force change through restrictive policies. When President Nixon took the dollar off the gold standard, he also imposed a trade surcharge and domestic wage and price controls. None of that worked, as history has shown. Today, fixing the current account deficit poses a similar challenge. It is very unlikely that any trade restrictions will help resolve this problem. It is more likely to require exchange rate adjustments, notably between the dollar and the euro; a drastic slowing of U.S. consumer demand (and credit-based spending); and a trend toward increased demand in other countries, which is beyond the control of U.S. economics, but an important part of the required change.

Can the United States make the majority of these adjustments at home? It's unlikely that a fix in the exchange rates between dollar and euro would start the process; it is more likely to occur as part of a shift in the trend. We should keep in mind:

> The historical experience of the United States, and of other industrial countries as well, has been that growth slows during periods of substantial external adjustment, in part, because of deliberate policy actions but in larger part via the endogenous process of adjustment. . . . Historically exchange rate crises have occurred well into the period of external adjustment rather than at their start. The increased flexibility of financial markets that Greenspan has identified may prove to be a double-edged sword.[23]

The great wild card in our economic future—the dollar—is the key to everything else.

With the persistent large current account deficit, the dollar's strength depends on the stock market at home, and on demand for goods and products overseas. In both of these cases, changes in trends are beyond Mr. Bernanke's control. As the Fed chairman should have found out by now, you can lower interest rates only so far and for so long. To continue to finance our debt-based economy, we'd require a new bubble. And it's probably not wise to peg our national economic health on the chances of a major bull market run-up in prices. It could happen, of course, but the bubble—like all economic bubbles— would not last forever. Eventually, the *real* problems are going to have to be addressed with *real* solutions.

We saw the dollar top out and then begin to fall against the euro, and that is going to continue—because, let us not forget, the dollar's strength has been borrowed. As the slide of purchasing power continues, trade deficits will get worse as well. This is what happened in the years 1985–1987 when the deficit rose very quickly even though the dollar's value virtually collapsed. The Federal Reserve's policies are both unrealistic and, in the long term, damaging. The agency still believes that continuing to increase credit is a worthy form of productivity expansion, and that ultimately it might even close the trade gap.

A DOLLAR APOCALYPSE?

Inertia is the rule of the day, unfortunately. That force works whether the inertia is helping or hurting. We can see three real problems coming down the road:

1. *Reduced foreign investment.* In August 2007 we saw a slowing down among foreign lenders as a sign that we're reaching our international credit limit. Indeed, once investors begin to worry about their chances of getting repaid, the first impulse is to cut off the credit line—whether across international boundaries or in the casino.

2. *Continuing slow foreign demand for U.S. goods.* The slow pace of demand for U.S. goods—often cited as the *cause* of the trade deficit—is not only an external problem. It is also a symptom of the poor competitiveness in the United States. The fix for that problem is to attack the trade and current account deficits through revised pricing internationally, which is no easy task.

3. *Unfavorable currency exchange rates.* As the dollar reacts to continued credit-based spending, attrition of the dollar is going to continue. This damages purchasing power not only in the retail mall or when traveling to Europe, but also for U.S. business capital investment.

In the situation where the dollar has fallen for several years, we meet up with some economic contrarians who anticipate a rally and unexpected growth in the dollar's value. That trade has been a profitable one for the better part of the time we spent writing this book. But a bear market rally alone will not make other facts disappear.

What about the trade and current account deficit, flat manufacturing record, growing consumer debt, and so on? Those have to be fixed and changed. We cannot depend on the simple event stimulus to solve our problems. When you're broke, you may buy a lottery ticket out of desperation, and once in while, someone beats the odds and wins big. But that Hail Mary pass does not work for the economy.

Magic doesn't just happen. It is created. We need to set things in motion if we expect the dollar trend to reverse. If we do nothing, then nothing will happen. No rabbits in hats, hankies in sleeves, or sawing ladies in half will magically make the dollar change its current course.

The risk we face today is far different from similar currency adjustments in the past. Today, the risk that the dollar will fall is logical. It is based on our exposure to risk in the trillions of dollars of foreign holdings in U.S. dollars (against U.S. liabilities held in euros). The exchange risk involved in this is significant. The expectation of a strong dollar (and by the same trend, a weak euro) is unlikely. It's more probable that the trend will continue: We will see a weakening dollar and a strengthening euro as our debt levels continue to rise under the Fed's economic plan.

We may also be kidding ourselves if we continue to believe that the fate of the dollar against other currencies is under the control of central banks. While foreign investment was originally centered in these banks, growing free investment even among countries of the old Communist bloc has changed everything. The dollar's fate is increasingly held in the hands of millions of fickle investors. Of the many bubbles created by Mr. Greenspan's extremely loose monetary policies, the potential for change caused by international investment herd mentality is severe; markets outside the United States are too small to absorb a large capital outflow as domestic investors seek to flee falling dollars. So what can you do to avoid losing during the demise of the dollar, and to position your assets to profit from it?

CHAPTER 7

ALAS, THE DEMISE OF THE DOLLAR

The tide of red ink underpins our bearishness on the U.S. dollar.
—Stephen Roach

The global economy is changing, and the U.S. dollar is on the front lines of change. When we take a look at history, we see how past events have affected everything. The Black Death created a devastating labor shortage throughout Europe for decades. Christopher Columbus' voyages turned trade upside down for hundreds of years. The industrial revolution moved economic power in ways that continue to affect economic balances to this day. And now we face another great shift, away from the U.S. dominance of world markets and toward new leaders—China and India.

The economic reality—a type of geography—is changing. As a consequence, real estate speculation in New York, Chicago, and Los Angeles may be replaced with more global interest in the new real estate markets—in Beijing, Shanghai, and Bombay. Who knows? We can only anticipate how changes will occur based on what we observe today. Does this mean the age of America is ending? No, it simply means that economic muscle will be flexed by someone else in the future. This is a trend. And like all trends, they are more easily viewed in historical perspective but harder to judge from their midst.

When we look at trends in dollar values, we can observe that incomes have not declined. That's great. But we also see that prices have risen faster than incomes. So with decreased buying power (caused by this disparity) we *have* seen a decline in income in terms of what really counts. It takes more dollars to buy the same thing (in other words, prices are higher) but incomes have not risen to meet that price inflation. That's what happens when the value of the dollar declines.

THE FALLING DOLLAR AND ITS EFFECT ON THE MORTGAGE BUBBLE

Economic history is a history of bubbles—and of bursts. The great disservice being done to Americans by the financial media is that they are not being offered the opportunity to learn from what is going on. They are losing buying power, but apart from a few painful spikes at the gas pumps and in grocery lines, it's invisible.

In the Great Dollar Standard Era, the problem is global. While there is, of course, more to it than just the value of the U.S. dollar, here is how it works:

1. The dollar's value falls due to Fed policy, liberal credit, and artificially low interest rates.
2. Eventually, we cannot afford to buy as many foreign goods.
3. Foreign manufacturers, unable to sell at previous levels, have excess inventory, which causes an inflationary outcome.
4. Foreign governments, in an effort to counteract this inflation, blame the fallen dollar for the problem and begin moving out of U.S. instruments.
5. As debt returns to the United States, our system is unable to absorb it. This creates more severe recession at home.

Fake Money Creates Fake Demand

The whole thing is connected. This is similar to what happened worldwide at the end of the 1920s. The worldwide depression had numerous aspects, but most notable among them were two things: a huge transfer of funds from World War I reparations, and far too much credit that went beyond the borrowers' ability to repay. All of that credit—essentially, funny money—also creates a fake demand. We see the effects of this policy in housing as severely as anywhere. The whole mess is traced back to the origin—a Fed policy encouraging debt spending as a means to artificially create the appearance of productivity. This Fed policy has included four aspects:

1. *The Fed lent money below inflation.* Fed lending rates have been far below inflation (even as measured by the consumer price index, not to mention any real inflationary measurements). In a very real sense, the Fed has lost money on these loans. When inflation is higher than the lending rate, it is a loss. Just as a business cannot stay open when it sells goods below cost, the Fed cannot continue to hold the view that it isn't real money. The point is, the money lent out at bargain rates is real credit, and that is corrupted when it is given away cheaply.

2. *The low interest rates created the mortgage bubble without any corresponding investment.* It is basic: If you borrow money to invest in productivity (new plants and equipment, for example) it is a profitable use of money. But those low interest rates have gone, instead, into cheap long-term mortgages. Current homeowners have refinanced, and many first-time buyers have gotten into the market because low rates make housing affordable.

3. *The mortgage bubble inflated the housing market in an exaggerated fashion, creating the illusion of equity.* All of that cheap money created two troubling changes in housing. First was higher demand for owner-occupied housing based on the low cost of borrowed money rather than on any real market forces. Second was the resulting equity buildup from rapid expansion of market value in residential property. But it was as fake as the low interest rates. Like all pyramid schemes, the whole thing is finally crumbling under its own weight. We do not have an endless supply of new home ownership demand; quite the contrary. The baby boomers mostly own homes already, and a smaller population of people coming into home ownership age will ultimately result in an oversupply of housing stock. As the mortgage bubble continues to burst, we can expect to see several consequences:

- *Defaults on existing loans.* As rates on variable mortgages rise right up to—and beyond—their cap rates, we are seeing many of those marginal loans go into default. Many Americans are barely able to afford the mortgage payments they are making based on low-interest qualification. But as the Fed finally faces reality and allows interest rates to rise, those variable increases are kicking in as well. Many existing loans will be defaulted as a result.

- *Reduced market value from oversupply of housing.* The oversupply in building suddenly became obvious in late 2007. Everyone now realizes that too many homes were built too quickly, and the anticipated demand simply isn't there. The result: Those sky-rocketing market values are disappearing.
- *Abandonment of no-equity properties.* The reduced market value in homes is not going to be limited to a simple supply-and-demand cyclical change. For investors, reduced demand and flat or falling prices may be viewed as a cyclical and natural effect. But when the supply-and-demand cycle has been manipulated through interest rate policy, we have to expect a more wrenching effect. For those who entered into the housing market when prices were inflated, the day has finally arrived when they realize that real equity is below zero. There remains no incentive to con-tinue making payments, notably when lenders are raising rates *and* when the dollar's buying power is tumbling. In such a severe condition, marginal buyers are going to simply walk away from their properties. Why stay when there is no equity—or worse, minus equity?
- *Secondary market fallout from these changes.* Where did all of that mortgage debt end up? It isn't held by your local bank or sav-ings and loan. It got sold to Ginnie Mae, Freddie Mac, and other mortgage pools, which then packaged it up and sold it on to investors, many of them from Europe and Asia. Anyone who's been reading the news lately knows how those pools performed as the foreclosure rate rose and—at the same time—market values fell. A high rate of foreclosures in an over-built market is spelling disaster in the housing sector. While a normal supply-and-demand cycle may last three to five years on average, this downturn could be severe, going much longer into the future. The actual length of the housing recession will

depend on how decisively the Fed is willing to act and to fix the problem.

But the estimated 2.3 million homeowners facing disastrous rate resets through 2008 can't expect unconditional help from the Fed, as details of its compromise with the credit industry revealed in early December 2007. Under the terms proposed by President Bush and Treasury Secretary Henry Paulson, 1.2 million subprime borrowers in danger of losing their homes could be eligible for a five-year rate freeze. Emphasis is on the word *could:* Analysts from Barclays and the Center for Responsible Lending estimated that only between 145,000 and 240,000 borrowers will actually qualify for the freeze.

4. *The lack of investment and a flat manufacturing trend are damaging the U.S. competitive position in the world market.* Imagine an economic situation in which enterprising homeowners refinanced their homes when rates fell, invested the money in small business expansion, and created an internationally competitive economic climate. Well, this is the rosy picture the Fed hopes will eventually emerge from its monetary policies. By artificially lowering interest rates and enabling homeowners to get at their equity, the idea is that on a broad range of economic trends (housing, business investment, savings, etc.) there will be a strong growth spurt, an economic recovery that will return the United States to its leading position. But the lack of investment is doing great damage. The whole thing is credit-based, starting with the Fed losing on below-inflation loans and ending up with credit-based spending but no real productivity.

It appears that Fed policy was premised on the idea that lower interest rates would bring down inflation. Yet there is no evidence of that in economic history. It has always been an effective policy to raise rates to slow down inflation, just as lead rods are moved into the radioactive core of a reactor to cool down the chain reaction. Higher rates put a damper on spending. This has been recognized widely, so the Fed policy—based on the idea that lower rates are "good for the economy"—is without merit. In fact, it is damaging. The housing market and its mortgage bubble—and now, the subprime mortgage mess and the credit crisis—are most likely to be the first victims of this policy, and the most visible.

THE FALLING DOLLAR AND THE TRADE DEFICIT

It is difficult to look at jobs, inflation, and trade or budget deficits separately; they are all connected. For example, the trade deficit damages our ability to maintain a competitive international buying power, and until recently, that has only been visible to people traveling outside of the United States. Even then, the problem has not been viewed as a domestic problem. "It costs so much more to travel in Europe; prices have gone way up" is the tourist's lament. But why?

Here at home, we see no immediate evidence of the causes. Inflation is reportedly low, interest rates have certainly been down, and reports of a falling dollar have had no apparent effect on most people.

Our trade deficit is at $759 billion and growing. This is equal to less than 1 percent of U.S. assets, so it is understandable that some people discount the importance of the trade problem. But the trade deficit is not just a problem of Americans importing more goods than we export, or of paying for those goods on credit. It also includes what is happening overseas.

China, as well as other nations, is quietly building up its manufacturing base—and not just in cheaply made stuff like houses, shoes, or scarves. The Chinese didn't make any laptop computers in the 1990s, but by 2005 they were making about half of all laptops used in the world. The U.S. produces almost no denim jeans; Levi Strauss has closed all of its 60+ plants and moved operations to China. Even tech support is gone. Anyone with a Dell computer has already discovered that service reps have been moved from New Haven to New Delhi. The trade deficit is not just an accounting problem; it demonstrates— and vividly—that we are losing the competitive war for productivity.

The loss of jobs in these manufacturing plants is not *just* a loss of jobs. Economic efficiency and cheaper labor also spell the loss of entire industries. In exchange for lower prices, we consolidate, replace, and remove. For example, in 1910 the United States had more than 200 auto manufacturers.[1] Today there are only three, and they have become multinational.

United States trade history has been long and impressive. But the creation of national wealth was always based in *investment* in infrastructure. The creation of canals and railroads as the major means for moving goods from place to place in the nineteenth century was also the foundation of the U.S. world domination in trade. So what went wrong?

Some perspective is helpful. The United States started the nineteenth century as a young nation with no unified currency system, no economic policies to speak of, and—most notably—virtually no industry. But by 1885, the country was the world's leading manufacturer, creating nearly one-third of all goods worldwide (ahead of Britain and Germany in second and third place). This change was incredible. America held onto this dominance for the next 100 years, but things began to change in recent history. Why?

To understand this answer, we need to look at the differences between nineteenth-century and twentieth-century conditions. The United States in the 1800s was able to accumulate great economic power that it used to fund investment. The power came from some notable industries, specifically cotton, which was as indispensable to the world in those days as oil is today. The United States produced more than 80 percent of the world's cotton by 1860—a period when cotton fabric and its availability bolstered U.S. wealth. The agricultural industry of the South was supported by the use of natural resources in the United States, notably the discovery of gold in California. That defined U.S. wealth from 1849 forward (note how quickly the California territory was rushed into statehood after that discovery). Gold production exploded. In 1847, only 43,000 fine troy ounces were produced in the United States. By 1856, the number had risen to 2,661,000 ounces.[2]

The country's history and economic success grew out of its wealth in commodities like cotton and gold. But more significantly, that wealth was *invested* by the United States during the nineteenth century. It developed a steel industry, primarily with the incentive of building a national system of railroads. It also invested heavily in the development of canals.

It was railroads and canals together that enabled the United States to expand, both geographically and politically. This is often overlooked today. Few people see the agricultural and railroad industries as terribly exciting now, because their age has passed. In the 1820s and 1830s the United States undertook the ambitious project of the Erie Canal, which reduced travel time between the industrial middle of the country (Detroit and Cleveland, for example) and New York to 10 percent of the previous time. The Welland Canal later opened up the Great Lakes to the East Coast via water. Canal bonds were issued everywhere as various states went on a mission to build canals wherever they had bodies of water to connect. The whole movement revolutionized transport and the cost and time of moving goods to market.

Railroads achieved the same thing across the Great Plains and, ultimately, all the way to the Pacific. In 1820, only a few hundred miles of rail track were in use. By 1880, 120,000 miles had been put to work, with rail growth approaching 13,000 miles of new track per year.[3] The completion of the transcontinental railway was accompanied by high levels of speculation in the financial markets, which is no surprise. The railroad industry was by any measurement the biggest U.S. industry up to the 1920s. This brings us to a comparison with modern history.

The development of the great railways and canals in the nineteenth century was an investment in infrastructure. Even though investors and speculators often lost their money—most railroad stocks failed, after all—the development of rail transport was the centerpiece of U.S. domination of world manufacturing, a position it maintained throughout most of the twentieth century.

THE FALLING DOLLAR AND GROSS DOMESTIC PRODUCT

As a consumer of financial information, you should be disturbed at the confusion over exactly what gross domestic product (GDP) means and how it works. We like to joke in *The Daily Reckoning* that because GDP measures debt-fueled consumption, it really measures only the rate at which the United States is going broke.

To define GDP in some real terms, it should be thought of as the cash flow we generate from our assets. Just as a business uses cash, inventory, accounts receivable, and other working capital to fund its operations, a nation depends on its gross national product to fuel production. This is not only a U.S. problem. The fast-growing Chinese economy also faces growing GDP problems. Unfortunately, because China has largely pegged its currency to ours, both economies are joined at the hip—economically speaking.

China and the United States differ in how each country uses its debt, and this has a direct effect on GDP, of course. China is investing in development of a manufacturing economy, whereas the United States has become a consumer nation rather than a producer nation. This does not mean there are not serious problems. China is one of the highest-debt nations in the world today. Its latest reported debt (2004) of about $400 billion (U.S.) is about 23 percent of its GDP. While not as high as some other nations (e.g., Japan at 148 percent or Italy at 121 percent), the *real* numbers should be adjusted to include the obligations of state-owned businesses and banks. This takes China's total real debt to over half of its GDP.[4]

So the United States is not the only nation with a GDP problem. But is China's problem our problem? If we look at history, we will see another reason why China's growing debt will ultimately affect the U.S. dollar.

Since 1971, it has been U.S. economic policy to try to curtail its economic problems (the triple whammy of unemployment, inflation, and federal budget deficits) by increasing currency in circulation. Of course, this policy has the opposite effect. Just as the infamous Nixon wage and price controls failed, so does a policy based on solving problems by printing more fiat money. The United States, by leaving the gold standard, forced a readjustment in the currencies of all other trading partners. This affected GDP, of course; but more important, it affected the value of the dollar. Today, we see a growing debt in China as a percentage of its GDP and we have to wonder: Will the Chinese go down the same road, perhaps even to the point where their dominance in manufacturing will allow them to impose further devaluation on the United States?

China may be able to survive its current debt problem because that debt is being used to build productivity, thus future wealth generation. The debt is used for investment. This is not the case in the United States, where we have abandoned not only the gold standard, but also any hope of controlling inflation through monetary policy. The concept that printing more money (in other words, increasing debt) will solve our problems is a symptom of our waning GDP and economic competitiveness. If, indeed, China is destined to become the next economic power in the world, it will be the Chinese economy and not ours that dictates everything: prices, trade gaps, and ultimately the value of the dollar.

At the current rate, Americans will face inflation in the future. As we have said before, we need to understand that *inflation* is only another word for what is really going on, the falling purchasing power of the dollar. It is not accurate to go along with the theme that "a dollar is always worth a dollar, but inflation results when businesses raise prices." In fact, it is the decline in the dollar's value that leads to higher prices. It would be more accurate to define inflation as "a reduction in purchasing power of the dollar." Instead of deceiving ourselves by saying that "prices are up 10 percent over the past year" it would be more meaningful if we simply acknowledged that "last year's dollar is worth 90 cents today."

Traditional economic theory tells us that there are four causes of inflation. The money supply increases, the goods supply decreases, money demand decreases, or the goods demand increases. This is a rather mundane explanation of supply and demand relating to goods and services. But let's focus on one important aspect among these four: the increase in the money supply as a cause of inflation.

It's not just the fact that the Fed has put excess currency in circulation that is adding to the problem. It's more international than that. It's the blank check of expanding credit that is creating the real inflation, seen as lost purchasing power of the dollar. In other words, we could print money at the same pace and remain on the gold standard. However, the leverage of currency in circulation above real gold reserves would represent ever-growing risks. So we would be inhibited from infinite money printing by the degree of leverage. Foreign banks would also be aware of the growing disparity between currency in circulation and gold reserves, and *that* would serve as a market force controlling the value of the dollar and other currencies. Without the gold standard, we have nothing on which to base valuation—except the economic forces at work through GDP in the United States and China, the federal budget deficit, and the domestic credit purchasing trend. Finally, the lack of any growth in manufacturing in the United States will determine the dollar's value (i.e., real inflation) no matter how much currency the Fed puts into circulation.

We are reminded of what occurred in prewar Germany. In 1935, Adolf Hitler wanted to build up the military in defiance of the Treaty of Versailles. Although the country was broke, his economics minister,

Dr. Hjalmar Schacht, was instructed to find a way to finance a big-scale arms buildup. Schacht devised IOUs guaranteed by the German state. These debts were not included in any budget numbers, in published reports by the Reichsbank (the national bank of the government), or anywhere else. They were simply deficit spending, called MEFO bills, an abbreviation of *Metall-Forschungsgesellschaft* (a consortium of four armaments firms). Between 1935 and 1938, rearmament to the tune of $12 billion was funded through the sale of MEFO bills.[5]

The Schacht device is really no different from the U.S. Fed's policy of debt-based spending. So the U.S. GDP, based on spending rather than on investment, has a precedent in history. One could at least argue that a war economy has a version of investment to it. With the aim of taking over the economy and resource base of other countries, one motive for going to war has always been economic. So perhaps the justification for MEFO bills was that they represented an investment in future profits. As evil as Nazi Germany was, this argument at least provides some economic rationale. However, what is the equivalent in the United States? How will credit-based economic growth (that is, creating and maintaining GDP with credit in place of productivity) compete with countries like China, where aggressive expansion of a manufacturing base is heading toward dominance of the world trade market? There appears to be no economic rationale for the policy.

THE IMPACT OF A DECLINING DOLLAR

In the first edition, we said that the day was surely coming when foreign investors will reach a limit in their willingness to buy U.S. debt, thus financing our deficit. The finance minister of India hinted as much in late 2004. South Korea, too, made overtures for reducing the amount of U.S. dollars it holds in reserve. Well, that day has finally arrived. In August 2007, the central banks of Japan, China, and Taiwan sold U.S. Treasuries at the fastest rate in as many as seven years. Taiwan cut nearly 9 percent of its Treasury holdings, its biggest sell-off since 2000. China shed more than 2 percent, its biggest move since 2002. And Japan dumped 4 percent of its U.S. Treasuries, its largest reduction since 2002.

In all, Asian banks dumped about $52 billion in U.S. Treasuries in the final weeks of summer 2007. Not a gigantic sum, considering they own about $1 trillion more, but indicative of a trend.

A few months later, in November, the U.S. Treasury's TIC data revealed that Japan, China, Caribbean banking centers, Luxembourg, Hong Kong, South Korea, Germany, Singapore, Mexico, Switzerland, Turkey, Canada, the Netherlands, Sweden, France, Russia, Ireland, and Israel were all net sellers of U.S. Treasuries in September. For three months in a row, Japan and China—the world's largest holders of U.S. government debt—were sellers of such Treasuries. They now hold less than $1 trillion in dollar reserves. The central banks of these countries will conclude that it's smart to move their funds into other currencies—or to demand higher returns on their money.

We have all heard of *denial*—that self-protective tendency to contradict the obvious truth. Well, our federal policy makers are suffering from denial. Drunk on the power of the dollar and heedless of the damage it does to print more and more currency, our leaders have convinced themselves of something: that if the dollar's value falls, that will eliminate the trade deficit, reduce inflation, and improve our GDP. Just as onetime fiscal conservative Richard Nixon decided to try wage and price controls to solve the economic problems of 1971 and then took the U.S. economy off the gold standard, this new but illogical plan will also fail.

The United States has seen no growth in manufacturing (defined in terms of number of jobs, output, or profits) in more than 10 years. Changing this situation is the only solution to the trade deficit. In other words, we have to compete. We cannot trick the economy into coming into line by reducing the value of the dollar. It was possible on the gold standard to control economic trends to a degree. But we cannot simply look for easy solutions. Destroying our own currency's buying power is not the answer.

In fact, before we actually lost our trading dominance, the dollar wasn't worth too much compared to other currencies. Nixon's economic decisions were based on the realization that some prices were unrealistically low, coupled with the fear that not correcting that problem could cost him reelection. Unfortunately, he did not stop with wage and price controls and a tariff surcharge. He proceeded as though the problem had been created by the dollar, and that simply was not the case.

Between 1984 and 1994, total consumer credit in the United States grew from $527 billion to $1.021 trillion (almost doubling in the decade). From 1994 through 2007, the debt rose to $2.480 trillion, doubling again at an accelerated rate. Check the graph in Figure 7.1.

In the years from 1984 to 1994, the average annual growth in consumer debt was $49.4 billion per year. In the next decade, though, the average rate was $108.3 billion, and moving upward year after year at that faster rate. In the third quarter of 2007, consumer debt pushed close to $2.5 trillion—a 25 percent increase in less than three years. But that's only the tip of the proverbial iceberg: The real danger lies in the credit crisis beneath the surface.

That's the image that came to mind with the news a few days after Thanksgiving 2007 that Freddie Mac, Fannie Mae's more heavily exposed brother, halved its quarterly dividend and announced it would sell $6 billion of its own stock. Freddie had already posted a $2 billion loss—three times what analysts had expected—and then disclosed that it needed to raise more capital to meet regulatory requirements. To do that, Freddie cut its dividend by 50 percent. Freddie's accounting department already whacked the stock 50 percent at the beginning of November.

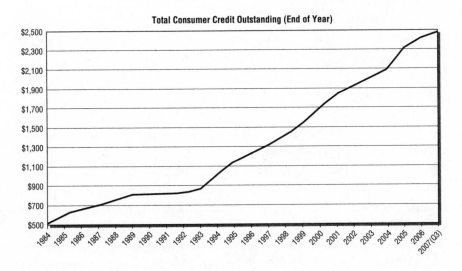

FIGURE 7.1 Consumer Credit Outstanding, 1984–2007

(*Source:* Federal Reserve.)

It's eerie—in December 2004, we ran the playfully facetious headline, "The Total Destruction of the U.S. Housing Market." Little did we know how right we were.

The crux of our argument at the time was that Fannie Mae, the nation's biggest—and government-backed—enabler of the subprime mortgage market, was in trouble. Internally, it had published a report revealing the firm's exposure to the derivatives market. The author of the report was reprimanded and fired, and the report mysteriously disappeared from the Internet. Fannie had been engaged in Enron-style accounting. Heck, it even used Arthur Andersen as its accountant—the same firm used by Enron. Congressional hearings followed, but all was soon completely forgotten—until the news surfaced about the fallout with Freddie.

Until the secondary market for mortgage-backed securities started drying up over the summer of 2007, Freddie Mac and Fannie Mae—which own or guarantee about 40 percent of the $11.5 trillion residential mortgage market in this country—were the reliable sources of credit that kept a pulse beating. Now Freddie is telling us that if conditions continue to deteriorate, it may have to purchase fewer mortgages, which would take even more homebuyers out of the market.

As if on cue, the worst home sales report of all time was issued the same day. Existing home sales fell 20 percent in October from the previous October, to an annual rate of 4.9 million, the lowest ever recorded by the National Association of REALTORS® (NAR). October also marked the 15th out of the past 17 months in which this price measure posted a year-over-year decline. And wouldn't you know—a record level of homes are now sitting in inventory, a whopping 11-month supply.

Given the massive acceleration in rate of credit expansion, it does not seem likely that a falling dollar is going to fix the problem of the trade deficit. This credit money, which is not backed by anything, can best be described as "magical, out-of-thin-air fairy dust money."[6] One saving grace in today's economy is that our trading partners and competitors are in bed with us, economically. In the 1980s, overseas dollar-based assets held by foreign interests were practically at zero. Today, those holdings have ballooned to about $16.295 trillion. So our fortunes—including the value of the dollar—have ramifications for heavily invested foreign central banks and private interests.

THE THREAT OF INFLATION

The United States has enjoyed such low inflation for many years (compared to the late 1970s, at least) that many Americans believe that inflation has ended. Ironically, some people even credit the Fed and its monetary policies with controlling or ending inflation.

This is 180 degrees from the truth. We have inflation, but the credit-based economy and liberal monetary policies of the Fed have kept it pent up. Experience and history both tell us that these aberrations eventually become realized, usually with a vengeance.

We have to remember that inflation and the falling dollar are in fact the same thing, but expressed in different ways. So the Fed's policies are designed to keep interest rates and inflation down while encouraging consumer debt to rise—all on the premise that this will stimulate investment and growth. At the same time that the Fed wants to continue to see a falling dollar, it claims it is fighting to ward off inflation. This makes no sense.

Or perhaps it does make sense—if we listen to Mr. Bernanke, at any rate. He has a way of framing bad news that is reminiscent of many corporate annual reports. This mentality—that news must always be expressed in positive tones—tends to obscure what is really going on. To make this point, some years ago a small medical instruments company had suffered several years of ever-growing net losses. In its latest report, the letter from the chairman had to explain away an even higher loss than previous losses—in spite of belt-tightening promises. His statement was, "The reduction in the rate of increases in net losses underscores our move toward profitability."

Amazing. But this is how a lot of corporate matters are reported, as anyone knows upon reading these promo pieces from the chairman and CEO . . . which brings us back to Mr. Bernanke.

In December 2006, he traveled to Beijing to talk to the Chinese about their economy. Bernanke duly noted China's "impressive rate" of growth, of 9 percent a year from 1990 to 2005.[7] But that's nothing compared to the growth in trade that occurred after China joined the World Trade Organization in 2001, when the dollar value of exports started growing at an average annual rate of about 30 percent. Add in capital inflows—particularly foreign direct investment (FDI), which leaped from $2 billion in 1986 to $72 billion by 2005—and you're looking at a pretty robust picture.

But there's a flaw, Bernanke told his audience: The Chinese are investing and saving too much. Approximately 33 percent of their GDP goes into fixed business investment, and the national savings rate is way into the ozone, at 52 percent—compared to our now below-zero rate. That kind of behavior is contributing to "global imbalances," the Fed head told the Chinese gravely. The solution: Increase monetary and social policies "aimed at increasing household consumption." In other words: Get debt.

It's amazing just how much Bernanke—dubbed the "un-Greenspan" when he first took over at the Federal Reserve—sounds like his old boss. In fact, Greenspan set the stage for everything we're seeing and hearing from Bernanke. To understand just how much, it's helpful to reread Greenspan.

In January 2004 Mr. Greenspan explained that our trade gap with China (while still a deficit) had narrowed. He explained that "following a shortfall of $41.6 billion a month earlier . . . the trade deficit with China narrowed to $10.8 billion from $13.6 billion."[8]

Great news, Mr. G. The Fed chairman's policy of "salvation by devaluation" was reflected momentarily in reduced trade gap numbers. But are these truly related? While reducing the dollar's value is unavoidably inflationary (by definition, a lower dollar *is* inflation), it boggles the mind to accept Greenspan's argument. In essence, he claimed that inflation creates lower trade deficits. He has never admitted that a devalued dollar and inflation are the same animal, but anyone who has survived an Economics 101 class knows that it is. We have cleaned up inflation by calling it something else. We have put lipstick on the pig and called it by another name.

In fact, Greenspan shrugged off concerns about the falling dollar. He has said that he expects current global currency imbalances will be easily diffused with little or no disruption.[9] He referred to flexibility in international policy as the key to this easy fix. On January 13, 2004, Greenspan spoke in Berlin: "The greater the degree of international flexibility, the less the risk of a crisis."

He also set up the European economies as the fall guy for the effects of the falling dollar, thus a rising euro, saying that any protectionist initiatives among European nations would erode the flexibility.

In the same talk, Greenspan—perhaps in a fit of denial?—commented that U.S. current account deficits were not a problem. Here again, he obscured the relationship between a falling dollar and inflation, stating that it was true the U.S. dollar had fallen against other nations' currencies, but at the same time inflation "appears quiescent."

Mr. Greenspan's cryptic warning concerning where this all goes contradicts his claim to a quiescent inflation. He went on to explain that if the current deficit were allowed to continue, "at some point in the future further adjustments will be set in motion that will eventually slow and presumably reverse" demand from foreign investors for U.S. debt, a prediction that looks very possible lately.

At that time, the U.S. trade deficit sat at about 5 percent of GDP. Greenspan shrugged this off as well, even in the face of rising deficits over time. He claimed that financing the U.S. debt with U.S. dollars would, in essence, expand the U.S. ability to carry debt. Or, putting it another way—if we understood Mr. Greenspan correctly—our dollar is so popular that it serves to increase our international line of credit. This sounds like the policy of deficit spending—no big deal, apparently—should only continue and expand.

In fact, Greenspan's opening statement during his January 2004 speech is amazing in itself:

> Globalization has altered the economic frameworks of both developed and developing nations in ways that are difficult to fully comprehend. Nonetheless, the largely unregulated global markets do clear and, with rare exceptions, appear to move effortlessly from one state of equilibrium to another. It is as though an international version of Adam Smith's "invisible hand" is at work.[10]

The "invisible hand" was Adam Smith's metaphor referring to an economic principle of "enlightened self-interest." The theory supports a contention that in a capitalist system, the individual works for his own good, but also tends to work for the good of the nation or community as well:

> Every individual necessarily labors to render the annual revenue of the society as great as he can. He generally neither intends to promote the public interest, nor knows how much he is promoting it. He intends only his own gain, and he is in this, as in many other

cases, led by an invisible hand to promote an end which was no part of his intention. Nor is it always the worse for society than if it was no part of his intention. By pursuing his own interest he frequently promotes that of the society more effectually than when he really intends to promote it. I have never known much good done by those who affected to trade for the public good.[11]

Greenspan latched onto this argument, made originally by Smith to argue against regulation and protectionism in markets. But the unintended consequences of the principle are disturbing if, as Mr. Greenspan claims, the international monetary situation depends on governments doing less rather than more. The Fed chairman had more praise for Adam Smith a year later in the Adam Smith Memorial Lecture in Fife, Scotland. He described Smith as "a towering contributor to the development of the modern world." He expressed the belief in Smith's principles of an unregulated market, in an apparent reference to modern trends in international trade and notably China. Greenspan said, "A large majority of developing nations quietly shifted to more market-oriented economies."[12]

Let's not forget, it was the United States that went off the gold standard—arguably to remove the restrictive nature of pegging money to gold, but in practice to enable a planned intervention in international trade by expanding the dollar. That in itself was and still is a form of protectionism, the very thing Greenspan argued against. If U.S. policy was truly faithful to the idea of unregulated international monetary policy, it would have left the gold standard in place, recognizing it as a means for curtailing runaway inflation, jarring monetary disparities, and—as we now have—huge deficits. In spite of the Fed theme to the contrary, printing money and creating a debt-based economy is contrary to Smith's hypothesis.

Greenspan had a theory about the huge U.S. current account deficits. But he dismissed it in one respect by pointing out that deficits and surpluses always balance out:

> Although for the world as a whole the sum of surpluses must always match the sum of deficits, the combined size of both, relative to global gross domestic product, has grown markedly since the end of World War II. This trend is inherently sustainable unless some countries build up deficits that are no longer capable of being financed.[13]

Hmm. As in the case of the United States perhaps? What Greenspan is saying here is that growing deficits are no problem unless they get so large that the lender nations—those with net surplus dollars—are no longer willing to carry the debt. This is clearly the simplest method by which to judge a nation's economic health. If the size of the current account deficit has gotten too large, it is easy to see that the country is living beyond its means—and the trend cannot continue without dire consequences. However, it appeared that Mr. Greenspan was not aware of this. He continued:

> There is no simple measure by which to judge the sustainability of either a string of current account deficits or their consequences, a significant buildup in external claims that need to be serviced. In the end, the restraint on the size of tolerable U.S. imbalances in the global arena will likely be the reluctance of foreign country residents to accumulate additional debt and equity claims against U.S. residents.[14]

In fact, as Greenspan pointed out in the same speech, the trend is certainly heading to that obvious but dire conclusion. He noted that by the end of 2003, net external claims had grown to about 25 percent of U.S. GDP, with average annual growth continuing at 5 percent per year. But, he contends, "the sustainability of the current account deficit is difficult to estimate." Why, we wonder, is it so difficult? Greenspan double-speaks by explaining that U.S. capacity for increased debt is "a function of globalization since the apparent increase in our debt-raising capacity appears to be related to the reduced cost and increasing reach of international financial intermediation."[15]

Well, that statement makes no sense, but here's what really matters. Any American who holds a mortgage knows where it goes if he or she keeps borrowing on the equity. Your bank wants you to have 20 percent equity in your home, for example; but you sign up for a series of additional mortgages, a line of credit, and refinancing of your paper equity. At some point your debt is 125 percent of equity, and then what? Will your lender institute some form of "financial intermediation" by saying, for example, "no more debt"? If a lender draws the line at that point, then your capacity to borrow will be stopped. This is where the U.S. debt trend is going, and Greenspan admitted as much in the statement (even though no one can be sure about what he really meant).

Greenspan seemed to earnestly believe in his theme, that "market forces" would work in a flexible world economy to make everything all right. Does this mean the deficits will simply disappear? No, but it does imply that the *level* of deficits is acceptable given those very market forces—and that these levels will become even more acceptable in the future. Somehow. It's a matter of *flexibility* in his view that will lead to this improvement in the state of U.S. debt. He said:

> Can market forces incrementally defuse a worrisome buildup in a nation's current account deficit and net external debt before a crisis abruptly does so? The answer seems to lie with the degree of flexibility in both domestic and international markets. By flexibility I mean the ability of an economy to absorb shocks, stabilize, and recover. In domestic economies that approach full flexibility, imbalances are likely to be adjusted well before they become potentially destabilizing. In a similar flexible world economy, as debt projections rise, product and equity prices, interest rates, and exchange rates could change, presumably to reestablish global balance.[16]

And if only the rest of the world would go along with U.S. policy in other regards, we could all have peace and prosperity. But that isn't going to happen. It's more likely that the invisible hand is going to slap us across the face with a monetary rude awakening.

Greenspan refers to the "paradigm of flexibility" in a stated desire to see exchange rates stabilize. But doesn't that sound like what Nixon was trying to accomplish in 1971 by going off the gold standard? To any extent, what he was trying to accomplish didn't work. It only led to the current mess in terms of the trade deficit and the falling dollar.

Greenspan's speech was revealing, not only in demonstrating his economic philosophy but also in showing his view of how economic forces work. His dismissal of growing debt as a significant force ignored the important differences between *spending* borrowed funds and *investing* borrowed funds. Apparently he didn't believe the distinction to be an important one, and neither does his successor. The problem is—and it's a big problem as 2007 draws to a close—the fiscal environment has changed. Inflation is much more of a threat, but Bernanke doesn't have the luxury of following in Greenspan's footsteps. In fact, Greenspan said so to *USA Today* in an interview published on September 14, 2007 to promote his autobiography. "We had the luxury of not worrying too much on the downside." But now, "That luxury is gone. So Ben [Bernanke] is going to have a tougher time, more difficult decisions, than I had."

INFLATION BY ANY OTHER NAME

If you define *inflation* as an expansion of the money supply (which, of course, devalues the dollar through dilution, at the very least), you need to also look beyond this definition. We are facing a new kind of inflation: *price inflation.*

Higher prices are a reflection of decreased purchasing power of our dollars. It is academic to argue which method of explanation is more accurate. Under widespread price inflation, it takes more money to buy the same stuff.

We should not ignore the extreme hyperinflation of Germany in the 1920s as an example of how bad things can become when inflation gets out of control. In January 1919 an ounce of gold cost 170 German marks. Less than five years later, the same ounce cost 87 *billion* marks. The hyperinflation affected everything, even postage stamps. For example, in 1923 a stamp originally issued for 300 marks was overstamped with a revised value of 2 million marks.[17] (See Figure 7.2.)

FIGURE 7.2 1923 Stamp Overstamped with Revised Value

We have seen a similar type of inflationary effect in many other countries. Toward the end of the USSR empire, a worker was interviewed in Moscow during a time when some employers were paying workers in clay bricks rather than currency. When asked about the situation, a worker told a reporter, "We pretend to work and they pretend to pay us."

A devalued currency—or, in the extreme, a worthless currency—is going to affect where and how we invest. It will affect far more than prices, perhaps requiring everyone—even the securely delusional American consumer—to rethink the whole attitude toward money, spending, and debt.

One important sign of the weakening dollar and currency inflation is seen in the price of gold. Tracking gold prices is a reliable way to gauge what is going on with currency values, because the tendency is for gold's value to rise as currency values fall. Gold rose above the magic $400 per ounce level in 2003 for the first time in eight years. By 2004, the gold price had grown 25 percent in one year and was up 60 percent from its low point in 1999. Almost as good as gold is the opinion of those in the know, such as Warren Buffett. In 2003, for the first time in his life, Buffett began buying foreign currencies—to the tune of $12 billion by year-end. He cited continuing weakness in the U.S. dollar as the reason.[18]

By the beginning of 2005, Buffett was still betting against the dollar. His foreign currency holdings increased to $20 billion. At the time he began buying up overseas currency, the euro was worth 86 cents to the U.S. dollar. By January 2005, the euro traded at $1.33, an improvement of over 50 percent; and it continued its upward climb. So is Buffett smart to change his strategy? In the first three quarters of 2004, his company, Berkshire Hathaway, netted $207 million on currency speculation—not bad. Looking back at the fall of the dollar against the euro—33 percent between 2002 and 2005—it would seem that Buffett's timing was great. Since 2002, he has scooped up $2.2 billion for his shareholders. In his famous plain-speaking way, he explained his concerns about the value of the U.S. dollar: "If we have the same policies, the dollar will go down."[19]

In fact, Buffett told us in person recently, "If the current account deficit continues, the dollar will be worth less 5 to 10 years from now."

"Insanity consists of doing the same thing over and over again and expecting a different result," the sage spake. "In the United States, the cause, in my view, of the declining dollar in very major part, is the current account deficit, and the trade deficit being the biggest part in that." He went on to say, "I don't know what it will look like in any short term, but I would say that force-feeding a couble billion a day to the rest of the world is inconsistent with a stable dollar."

In a Q&A session with the *Financial Post*, Buffett admitted he had made "several hundred million" bucks buying Canadian loonies over the past year, a position that he also admitted he regretted leaving.

Today, Buffett says he currently owns only two currencies: the embattled greenback and Brazilian real. The dollar, suffice to say, hasn't been treating him well. Buffett didn't disclose when he bought reals, so we can only guess how he's done on that one.

Buffett's change to foreign currencies is significant. When the Oracle of Omaha does something he has never done before, it's worth noting.

Why, though, has he decided on this big shift now? Buffett is concerned with the huge (and growing) balance of payments deficit. Foreign investors hold $9 trillion in U.S. debt, consisting of bonds and other debts. He sees the day in the not so distant future when this buying spree will end. Because the U.S. economy depends on continued overseas investment (as a means of financing our debt economy), any slowdown in the volume will result in further weakening of the dollar. In other words, it can't go on forever.

Buffett isn't the only guru who sees the problem in clear terms. George Soros, Sir John Templeton, Jim Rogers, and Bill Gates all agree. In other words, many investment luminaries known for their good timing and vision are in agreement that the dollar is in big trouble. In a nutshell, a weakened dollar is a relative matter, so it means that other currencies will perform better and will strengthen. Even Alan Greenspan knows that all things equal out, whether trade imbalances, deficits and surpluses, or currency values.

THE FED'S PREDICTABLE COURSE

Fed policy is, in fact, an intrinsic part of the path toward a falling dollar—not only by inevitable consequences, but as part of a stated federal policy. The Fed and the Bush administration want the dollar to fall as a perceived means for reducing debt. This is a new direction. In past economic practice, allowing interest rates to rise was the effective means for curbing excess spending. Today, the spending isn't viewed as a problem. The Fed seems to think that having further international credit cut off is the real threat.

A review of Fed history explains how we've gotten to this point.

The Federal Reserve was first suggested in 1907 by Paul Warburg, publisher of the *New York Times Annual Financial Review*. Warburg suggested the formation of a central banking system to help deter panics. One of Warburg's partners, Jacob Schiff, warned the same year that lacking such a central bank, the country would "undergo the most severe and far reaching money panic in its history."[20]

They were both right in their prediction. The infamous Panic of 1907 hit in October. The idea that panics were caused, at least in part, by lack of strong central banking controls continues to find considerable support. Even Milton Friedman (with Anna J. Schwartz) is on record in believing that the Great Depression was as severe as it was primarily because the Federal Reserve mismanaged the nation's money supply.[21]

Congress passed the Owen-Glass Act creating the Federal Reserve System, and the new bill was signed by President Woodrow Wilson on December 23, 1913.

We need to review the *responsibilities* of the Fed to understand where we are today. There are three primary roles the Fed was authorized to undertake: supervise and regulate banks, implement monetary policy by buying and selling U.S. Treasury bonds, and maintain a strong payments system. Operating as a central bank (organized with its 12 regional reserve banks, a Board of Governors, and the Federal Open Market Committee), the Fed has expanded beyond its original mandate. Consider the second and third roles: to implement monetary policy by buying and selling U.S. Treasury bonds and to maintain a strong payments system.

Today, the Fed certainly implements monetary policy. It controls interest rates as a means of determining the value of the dollar and—in spite of the rather restrictive original definition of how the Fed was to implement policies—it does much more today than buy and sell Treasury bonds. A "strong payments system" may have had a relatively restrictive meaning in 1913, and we have to wonder what members of Congress would have thought about the original bill if they could see our economy today. Given the widespread isolationist view in that period, it is doubtful that Congress would have been willing to give over the power to the Fed to influence currency exchange values throughout the world. It would have been interesting to see how differently U.S. monetary policy would have developed if the original bill had also tied the Fed's actions into a requirement that the United States remain on the gold standard. Alas, history is moved by conundrums. The dollar just happens to be one of the biggest, most challenging conundrums in financial history. And just happens to have come on our watch.

CHAPTER 8

CRISIS AND OPPORTUNITY IN THE TWILIGHT OF THE GREAT DOLLAR STANDARD ERA

Intractable problems are usually not intractable because there are no solutions, but because there are no solutions without side effects.

—Lester Thurow

When written in Chinese, the word *crisis* is composed of two characters. One represents danger and the other represents opportunity.

—John F. Kennedy

What is *real* money? This question should be on the minds of every investor and everyone who observes what happens at home and abroad. The U.S. government has done an excellent job of convincing us that all of those dollar bills being exchanged work as actual money. In fact, though, everyone knows they have no tangible value. They are backed only by (1) a promise by the government to honor the debt, and (2) assurances from the government that the money does have value, that one dollar is worth one dollar.

Both of these promises are questionable. How can the government promise to pay its debts when the total of that debt keeps getting higher and higher? It's already out of control. And in our fiat money system, the implied promise that a dollar is worth a dollar has to be looked at with suspicion as well.

This is not just an exercise in economic theory. The near future could prove to be a financial disaster for anyone who continues to have faith in the strength of the dollar. In fact, a collapse is inevitable and it's only a question of how quickly it is going to occur.

The consequences will be huge declines in the stock market, savings becoming worthless, and the bond market completely falling apart. As the value of the dollar falls, that dollar will no longer be worth a dollar; it will be worth only pennies on the dollar. It will be a rude awakening for everyone who has become complacent about America's invulnerability.

The monster lurking in the near future has been caused by government policy. Our leaders have allowed foreign interests to take control of our economic destiny, and we cannot necessarily count those foreign interests as allies. We are not threatened by imminent invasion or loss of freedom to move about; but the extravagant American standard of living is about to be changed, drastically and suddenly. This has come about by three changes in fiscal status. First, the strength of the dollar and the level of interest rates are no longer in the control of the Fed. Second, good jobs have been sent overseas, and the so-called recovery has consisted of low-paying jobs. Third, because average wages are falling, Americans cannot afford inflation; even with our increasing credit card and mortgage–based bubble economy, the illusion of prosperity cannot go on forever.

LOSS OF CONTROL OVER THE VALUE OF MONEY

The Fed has decided that nothing can ever stop the U.S. economy. Continued growth is inevitable and—the ultimate delusion—our officials appear to truly believe that they can control it. If the economy slows, no problem. The Fed has declared lower and lower interest rates as a means for encouraging more and more debt—and that is called sound policy.

It's not just the consumer who has spent beyond his means. The government has led the way by bad example. U.S. borrowing has expanded to the point that foreign central banks own major portions of the U.S. debt. The Bank of Japan held $668 billion of Treasury securities in 2004, compared to the Federal Reserve holdings of $675 billion. In other words, the Bank of Japan nearly matched the Fed in ownership of U.S. debt.[1] (Shortly after the first edition went to press, Japan began cutting its holdings, down to $582.2 billion as of September 2007—less than the debt the Fed owns, at $666.4 billion. If you just add in China, South Korea, and India, the Asian central banks own a lot more debt than the Fed does.)

With so many Asian currencies tied to the dollar, isn't it in their interests to keep dollar values high? Yes, but only to a point. Asian central banks will ultimately allow the U.S. dollar to fall to contain inflation in their countries. And the more debt those central banks control, the greater their control over the U.S. dollar—and over the standard of living in the United States.

Should we fear Asian inflation? In 2008, growth of gross domestic product (GDP) is continent-wide at an expected 9.8 percent, slightly less if you look at recent past performance in Vietnam (8.2 percent), Singapore (7.5 percent), Malaysia (6.1 percent), and South Korea (4.9 percent). The surprise is China, where growth is expected to slow down from 10.8 percent to 9.8 percent in 2008. With the exception of Japan, which is struggling at 1.5 percent, my point is real GDP growth in these countries is two and three times ours in the United States.

Ultimately, these trends will lead to inflation, and the best way to fight inflation is to let your domestic currency grow in value. And here is where large holdings of U.S. debt become important. Because Asian central banks hold such vast sums of U.S. debt, they can also control the value of the dollar.

We are now seeing a trend in Asia toward buying fewer U.S. dollars and then selling the holdings they already have, as well as selling off U.S. bonds. All of these changes will force the U.S. dollar to fall and interest rates to rise here at home. In other words, Asian inflation is held in check and transferred into U.S. inflation. This will ultimately be the price the United States will have to pay for allowing its federal and consumer debt to get out of control.

So domestic interest rates are not really controlled by the Fed any longer. The fact that Asian central banks own such vast dollar reserves and hold so much debt means *they* will determine not only how much inflation takes place, but also *where* it takes place.

The trend toward dumping dollars and debt will have a direct impact on the U.S. stock market. Because the dollar has been falling in recent years, foreign investors in U.S. stocks—representing over 10 percent of the whole market—have been getting lower returns on their investments. When the dollar takes an even sharper turn south, those foreign investors will sell. That will mean that the supply of stocks will increase rapidly or, putting it another way, prices will plummet as foreign investors start dumping U.S. shares.

JOBS SENT OVERSEAS

The U.S. government likes to minimize the trend in outsourcing of jobs. They point to job numbers—the creation of millions of new jobs, especially in election years. But the sobering truth is far different.

The U.S. labor market has traditionally been defined by higher wages paid than in any other industrialized country. But the emergence of cheap production overseas means that companies are going to seek the most competitive labor source. Therefore, high-paying jobs in the U.S. are disappearing, and rapidly. The average American factory worker gets $17.25 per hour. In China, while wage rates vary by region, the average salary is still just $198 month—up dramatically from $105 a month just a few years ago. But you see the difference. With U.S. workers earning more in two weeks than Chinese laborers get in one year, our labor economy simply cannot compete. The Chinese economy—with millions of people looking for work—can afford to compete with U.S. wage levels by offering dirt-cheap pay, and there is an infinite supply glad for the work—even despite Chinese government complaints that wage rates are rising too quickly.

As a consequence of globalization, wages in the United States are flat. Wage levels are not growing at all. Of course, some isolated and highly specialized industries will continue to hold the edge in America but, on average, high-paying wages are being replaced overseas and our so-called job growth is in the lowest-paying industries. We see evidence everywhere. Almost no denim jeans are made in the United States anymore. Most of our clothing (95 percent of all footwear, for example) is imported from China and other Asian countries. More than half of all laptop computers are manufactured in Asia, and less than a decade ago virtually all of these were made in the United States.

What has brought about this huge change? We have to realize that the change is significant and has ramifications as great as any economic revolution. We must confront the fact that

> as a result of the breakdown of communist and socialist ideology and the end of isolationist policies on the Indian subcontinent—the world's economic sphere was enormously enlarged with close to three billion people joining our free-market, capitalistic system. The importance of adopting capitalism in countries like China, the former Soviet Union, Vietnam, and India cannot be underestimated and will again radically change global economic geography.[2]

Little discussion has been given on the impact of these three billion new capitalist competitors with the United States. It is, indeed, hard to fathom the overall impact of such a large shift in economic influence, but the shift is very real. The fact that U.S. jobs are being transferred to countries that were previously in the Communist bloc makes the point: As long as these countries were our enemies, there was no trade between us. Now that we are all trading partners, all of those people are a cheap labor pool.

The problem goes back to the Fed and its ill-advised monetary policies. Driving down interest rates has, more than anything else, caused the shift in jobs. We want to buy from foreign countries and we're content to do so with debt, especially as long as interest rates are low. Unfortunately, this has created *real* inflation throughout our economy, at least on the cost side. But on the wage side, we've seen no growth at all. And eventually, this disparity is going to backfire on the Fed and on the American consumer.

HIDDEN INFLATION IGNORES THE REALITY

With wages flat and prices starting to rise, something has to give. It's going to come to a head. Gas prices are increasing rapidly, cutting into the discretionary income of most American consumers. Think about where this is going to hurt the most. Three areas deserve special mention: gas prices, mortgages, and credit card debt.

1. *Gas prices.* That fill-up costing $17 or $18 only a few years ago has risen to $30 or $40 per tankful, and likely will go far higher before it settles down—above $100 a tank if you drive a monster SUV with a 30-gallon tank. That's a real bite out of anyone's budget. At the same time, with wages remaining flat and the dollar's buying power falling, the increased cost is even greater than the dollar-to-dollar comparison.

2. *Adjustable-rate mortgages.* More and more refinanced mortgages and first-time mortgages have been underwritten with dirt-cheap adjustable-rate mortgages. Even with annual caps on increases and life caps on the loans, many homeowners will not be able to keep up with their mortgage payments as higher rates begin to kick in. Remember, wages are flat but interest expenses are going to rise. So as previous factory workers' hourly wages fall from $17 down to $10, mortgage lenders will be sending out letters telling them their monthly payments are going up.

3. *Credit card debt.* As people move debt around from one card to another with overall balances growing month after month, it is possible to take advantage of low rates and special offers. These three-month no-interest or low-interest deals were great in the past because they allowed consumers to use so-called free money, at least for a few months. But what happens when those special deals start to disappear? Rates will rise, minimum payment levels will follow, and the free money will dry up. Credit card consumers will need to stop buying and to begin repaying their debt—at higher interest rates and using dollars of lower value.

The media continually parrots the idea that while the dollar is falling against other currencies, we have little or no inflation. Yet a devalued dollar is precisely the definition of inflation in one sense. But inflation can be defined in another way, too: Dollar values remain steady but prices rise. In reality, these are just different aspects of the same phenomenon: a reduction in purchasing power.

Every investor will naturally want to look for ways to protect assets in the coming changes we are going to see. But those who understand the problem will also recognize that there is a solution. It is going to be found in the recognition of a single reality:

As the value of the dollar begins to fall, a corresponding and offsetting rise in value of commodities, raw materials, and tangible goods will occur.

In the large view, this means that investors will do best in the coming fall of the dollar by looking for investments that will benefit from that trend. For those who want to remain in the mutual fund sector, several funds emphasize profits resulting when the dollar falls and commodities (such as gold) rise in value. In the next section, you will see how open-end funds, closed-end funds, and exchange-traded funds (ETFs) can be used defensively to create profits when the dollar falls. The fund approach can work equally well to take advantage of rising prices in oil and other commodities.

For the sophisticated investor willing to take greater risks, currency speculation and using options or financial futures can be highly profitable. But these specialized derivatives markets demand great skill and experience, not to mention superb timing.

THE SMART MONEY STRATEGY

The U.S. economy is vulnerable on so many fronts. Social emphasis is being placed on protecting ourselves against terrorists and the threats of nuclear and chemical attack. But perhaps an equally serious peril is being ignored: our dependence on Middle East oil, for example.

We face a shrinking dollar, growing federal debt, increasing trade gap, record-high consumer debt, mortgage bubble, rising oil prices, inflation, flat productivity, falling wages—all part of the same trend translating to financial vulnerability, of course. But this economic sword of Damocles[3] points the way to how everyone can change their investing mode, not only to avoid loss but to *maximize* their investment profits.

If you accept the suggestion that big changes are going to be coming in these arenas, how can you reposition assets without also increasing market risks? Most investors are not going to sell their equity positions and go short on stocks, sell options, or sell futures. It simply isn't within their profile to do so. The trick is to find ways to take advantage of the coming changes in smart ways, and there are several. The way you choose to change strategies should depend on your investing experience and knowledge, risk tolerance, and personal preferences. In seeking ways to reposition your portfolio, there are four major markets to keep in mind as places where you will want to either avoid long positions or seek ways to work against the trends: mortgage pools, oil, foreign investments, and gold.

Mortgage Pools

A few years ago, mortgage pools seemed like no-brainers. Fannie Mae and Ginnie Mae, among others, were formed to buy up mortgages from primary lenders, package them into pools, and sell shares to investors. Because these pools consisted of secured debt in owner-occupied homes, they were described as low-risk investments. Not anymore. Fannie Mae, caught tinkering with the books, started dropping off its high stock price levels. In 2004, when the stock fell from over $77 per share down to $64 by September, we predicted that there was more turbulence to come.

We were right, unfortunately. By early December 2007, Fannie Mae's share price had dropped down to $37 and change—half of 2004's value. And we may be right again in predicting that more bad news is on the way. On December 4, Fannie announced that it will sell $7 billion worth of preferred stock, and then cut its dividend 30 percent to gain capital throughout 2008.

Investors who understand the options market would be wise to look critically at mortgage pools and think about buying long-term puts. (These options rise as the underlying stock's price falls, so the long-term put would be a good position for future price declines.) Why? Think about what happened to mortgage pools when the mortgage bubble burst. The problem isn't the size of its assets, but its core capital. After third-quarter losses of $1.4 billion, the lender has only $2.3 billion above the requirement of $41.7 billion.

Many of those owner-occupied homes, financed with variable-rate mortgages, may prove both overpriced and overfinanced once the bubble bursts. Continual refinancing motivated by lower and lower interest rates may have created widespread exaggeration in appraised values. Is this possible? Of course. Lenders, always looking for profits from new loans and from refinancing, hire appraisers to look at properties. If the lender wants to write the loan, you can be sure the appraisal will come out at the level the bank wants, unless claimed value is simply so out of line that the appraiser can't force the numbers. But appraisers who are paid by lenders understand the game. If banks want to aggressively write mortgages, appraisers will play along.

The lenders churn those loans. They make their profit short-term and then sell the debt to Fannie Mae and other mortgage pools. These pools, potentially with growing numbers of loans granted based on inflated or exaggerated values, are packaged and shares are sold to investors. As interest rates begin creeping upward, the monthly payments follow suit, and many homeowners, only marginally qualified to begin with, will find themselves unable to keep up. If the market value bubble also bursts, many borrowers will find themselves with zero equity and even negative equity in their homes. The simple thing to do in that case is to just walk away. The consequence of this will be higher levels of foreclosures. Those properties, going on the market at discount, will further drag down housing values. While these outcomes will affect regional markets and not necessarily national averages, if the problems are widespread they could spell disaster in the housing market and in the mortgage pool industry.

Oil

The price of oil went over $50 per barrel more than once in 2004, and by 2005 it seemed inevitable that the price was going to continue upward—and it has, with levels within range of $100 per barrel. Remember, only three years before, barrel prices were down at the $20 range. The rise in prices was not as surprising as how quickly it occurred. The problem is not just the Organization of Petroleum Exporting Countries (OPEC)'s holding back on production, although that certainly plays a part in the big picture. A civil war in Nigeria, the fifth-largest U.S. supplier, has directly affected U.S. imports as well. Add to that the four hurricanes in 2004, which cut back about 11.3 million barrels of production in the Gulf of Mexico.[4]

We are also facing growing demand for oil from China. Its oil imports were up nearly 40 percent in 2006, and that growing demand is also driving up prices paid in the United States. Chinese industry demand for oil is experiencing the highest growth curve in the world today.

When oil consumption in China is projected forward only a few years, it is apparent that consumption is going to outpace any hopes of production's keeping up. We can safely assume based on the trend in both industrial and consumer use that China is going to be the major oil consumer in coming years. So there is no logical reason to expect oil prices to drop. Rising oil prices affect one-third of all U.S. companies in some way. They create a double whammy on corporate profits. First, they drive up operating costs, and second, higher prices lead to reduced consumer spending. So it isn't just oil; it's the whole economy and any industry using petrochemicals. These include construction, manufacturing, clothing, carpeting, and a vast number of other industries.

Increased demand affects oil prices as much as weather patterns, political problems, and of course the threat of terrorism. And there is little the United States can do to fix the problem. In 2005, Congress approved oil drilling in the Arctic National Wildlife Refuge (ANWR) in Alaska. But even this won't produce a drop of oil for at least 10 years. Additional drilling is not going to address the deeper problem. At current consumption rates, there is only enough oil remaining to meet current need levels for another 30 years. The relationship between oil discovery and production also looks quite dismal, as Figure 8.1 shows.

What can investors do to position their portfolios? Stocks in companies involved in oil drilling and exploration, as well as those supplying drilling ventures, will continue to be solid investment opportunities in the future. New demand for oil rigs and drilling will push profits and stock prices higher. With OPEC already producing at 95 percent capacity, it is hollow to blame OPEC's policies for shortages. The truth is, reserves are dwindling as demand grows. Evaluate the oil production and drilling industry. Look for stocks that will benefit as oil prices rise. For mutual fund investors, seek out energy and commodity funds. For the more advanced investor who is comfortable with options, consider buying long-term calls in oil-related sectors with the greatest growth potential. Consider the four major subsectors within the larger energy sector of the market: coal,

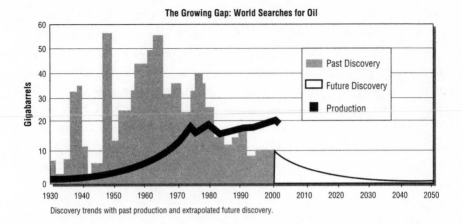

FIGURE 8.1 The Growing Gap: Oil Discovery versus Production, 1930–2050

(*Source:* Office of Science and Technical Information, Department of Energy, December 2004.)

oil and gas (integrated), oil and gas operations, and oil well services and equipment.

Of course, looking for energy-related mutual funds and ETFs is also a wise move. With prices rising, oil and gas companies and their products will become more in demand in the future.

Foreign Investments

Why invest overseas? Let's recall that China holds a huge amount of U.S. Treasury debt—not because it wants to per se but because holding U.S. debt gives China economic leverage over the United States in several ways. First, it ensures the continued trade gap favoring China and hurting the U.S. economy. Second, holding this debt enables China to virtually control U.S. buying patterns, interest rates, and economic policy. Third, China's currency is largely pegged to the U.S. dollar. If the dollar falls, so goes the yuan.

The more we buy from China, the more U.S. debt China acquires. This helps its producing economy while further damaging our consumer economy. What happens next? In the summer of 2007, China began selling off U.S. debt. This caused U.S. interest rates to rise as the Treasury was forced to find new lenders. For those investors anticipating this change, several smart moves are available. Three potential strategies offset the consequences of U.S.-China trade.

First, invest outside of the United States, either directly buying stocks or through ETFs. Seek investments in countries producing commodities and providing valuable resources, such as Australia. This continent is resource rich and geographically positioned to become a major supplier to China. Investing in Australia is a smart way to profit from China's growth without having to invest money in China itself.

Second, buy commodities by purchasing shares in corporations, index funds, or mutual funds specializing in the energy and commodities sector (oil and gas, precious metals, steelmaking). Third, use options to control large numbers of shares rather than buying shares directly.

Gold

The ultimate dollar hedge investment will always be gold. Investing in gold through ownership of the metal itself, mutual funds, or gold mining stock provides the most direct counter to the dollar. As the dollar falls, gold will inevitably rise.

In a moment, we'll provide you with many ways for positioning your portfolio to profit from a bull market in gold. For now, we emphasize the high probability of gold's future. The real potential for profits in the coming years and decades is not going to be found in the traditional American blue-chip industry. That is a financial dinosaur that can no longer compete in the world market. The future growth is going to be seen in gold. The world economy may remain off the gold standard, but ultimately the tangible value of gold as the basis for real value—whether acknowledged by central banks or not—will never change. Historically, this has always been the case, and it always will be. In other words, we are on a "gold standard" in spite of the popularity of fiat monetary systems.

Besides knowing where to position your capital to maximize returns when the dollar falls, also think about strategies that sell the dollar to produce profits.

HOW TO SELL THE DOLLAR

In 2004, then Treasury Secretary John Snow was traipsing about the globe trying to "talk the dollar down." Why? In a word: debt. At the time, our debt stood at $7 trillion, with interest payments in fiscal

2003 totaling $318 billion. But now the U.S. national debt stands above $9 trillion, with interest payments in fiscal 2007 adding $1.4 billion a day.

But the Fed and Treasury have engineered a strategy to pay off the debt with weaker and weaker dollars. And guess what? So far, so good. Since November 2002, the dollar has fallen against the euro more than 50 percent since its high in October 2000. Of course, this is not the first time we've gone through a managed devaluation of the currency. In the 34-year period since Nixon slammed the gold window shut and subsequently ended the Bretton Woods exchange rate mechanism, we've had only five major currency trends:

1. Weak dollar 1972–1978 (7 years)
2. Strong dollar 1979–1985 (7 years)
3. Weak dollar 1986–1995 (10 years)
4. Strong dollar 1996–2001 (6 years)
5. Weak dollar 2002– (? years)

The most notable period spanned the 10 years from 1986 through 1995. Then as now, the United States was fighting a historic current account deficit through managed debasement of its currency. But because the present bear market only began in February of 2002, the current cycle looks like it still has a number of years to run.

In the best-case scenario, if the current bear market follows the trajectory set by the 1986–1995 slump, we could see a weakening dollar for up to 10 years. This presents an opportunity for selling the dollar in one of four ways: direct and indirect speculations, using short- and long-term options for each. These plays will help you safely position your money outside the dollar bear market. And you stand to make a fair amount of money, too.

But there is great danger ahead. Since the trade deficit passed the $759 billion mark—6.3 percent of GDP—foreigners now must shell out about $1.5 billion a day just to keep the dollar afloat. And even during the managed dollar decline of 2003, the trade imbalance continued to grow. In 2005, Stephen Roach, Morgan Stanley's chief global strategist, predicted that the current account deficit at the time was on course to reach $710 billion—6.5 percent of GDP. He was short by only a few billion.

Herein lies the drama. The Bank of Japan spent the equivalent of $187 billion in 2003—and $67 billion in January 2004 alone—in a bid to prevent its strengthening currency from choking off the country's export-led recovery. In dollar terms, the Bank of Japan is now spending more than $1.5 billion every day trying to keep the yen from strengthening against the greenback.

Over a four-week period in the fall of 2003, combined foreign central bank purchases of U.S. securities topped $40 billion, more than $2 billion every trading day. Yet these central bank billions managed merely to limit the greenback's decline to just 2.3 percent over the same period. Can you imagine what would have happened if the banks hadn't pumped that money into the Fed's reserves? One former currency trader has asked, "If $40 billion cannot bring about even a minor rally, just how weak and despised is the once-almighty dollar?"[5]

We have relied on the kindness of strangers for too long. "We're like the untrustworthy brother-in-law who keeps borrowing money, promising to pay it back, but can never seem to get out of debt," Jim Rogers writes. "Eventually, people cut that guy off."[6]

There is no way the United States can possibly pay off its creditors should they decide to cash in their IOUs. Right now, the United States holds only about $70 billion in reserves against its obligations—much less than 2005's $87 billion. That would last about three minutes should creditors begin to sell the dollar, rather than trying to support it.

It's hard to imagine, isn't it? The world's reserve currency spiraling downward, out of control. But then, that's what the British must have thought in 1992 when they attempted to manage a devaluation of the pound. Despite the Bank of England's best efforts, sterling got away from them; the currency collapsed and Britain was kicked out of the Exchange Rate Mechanism (ERM) established to pave the way for the euro. On that day, known as Black Wednesday in Britain, currency speculator George Soros is rumored to have made as much as $2 billion. Don't be surprised if more fortunes emerge in the future as the dollar slips dangerously close to free fall.

By flooding the system with liquidity, the Fed cannot control the value of the U.S. dollar against foreign currencies; nor can they control its purchasing power—at least not indefinitely. The Fed's current policies can "give the majority of investors the illusion of wealth as asset markets appreciate," wrote Marc Faber in November 2003,[7] "while the loss of the currency's purchasing power is hardly noticed. This is particularly true of a society that has a very large domestic market, where 90 percent of the people don't have a passport and therefore know little about what is going on outside their own continent. And where the import prices of manufactured goods are in continuous decline because of the entry of China, as a huge new supplier of products with an extremely low cost structure, into the global market economy." If that's the case, you should look at any declines in the dollar as an opportunity to make some money.

The dollar is the single biggest element of risk in the world of finance today. Rearrange the current system of world finance ever so slightly, let confidence in the greenback falter, and the mighty dollar could go up in flames. There are many ways to hedge against this risk. Better still, there are many ways to profit from the likelihood the dollar will fall. Some methods are direct, some indirect. Some are leveraged, some unleveraged. There is a methodology for every taste, but before explaining the specifics, we ask: What ails the dollar?

The dollar is a victim of its own success. It is America's most successful export ever—more successful than chewing gum, Levi's, Coca-Cola, or even Elvis Presley, Britney Spears, and Madonna put together. Trillions of dollars flow through the global financial markets every week, and they are readily accepted at large and small—and clandestine—business establishments from Kiev to Karachi.

Today, there are simply too many dollars in circulation for the currency's own good. Why? Americans have been living beyond their means for more than two decades. The U.S. dollar's problems stem from a single cause. "If there's a bubble," wrote David Rosenberg, chief economist at Merrill Lynch, "it's in this four-letter word: debt. The U.S. economy is just awash in it."[8]

You've seen it firsthand: John Q. Public now holds more credit cards and outstanding loans—with a higher and higher total debt load—than ever before. Outstanding consumer credit, including mortgage and other debt, reached $9.3 trillion in April 2003—a significant increase from its $7 trillion total in January 2000—but by the third quarter of 2007, debt had nearly doubled since 2000, to $13.7 trillion. With consumer spending alone responsible for approximately 70 percent of U.S. GDP, that's quite a hefty personal debt load.

The corporate debt picture is no better. American companies have never depended so much on sales of their corporate bonds. Between 2002–2007, investment-grade corporate bond sales increased nearly 60 percent, growing from $598 billion to $951 billion. But junk bond sales for that same period broke the bank, surging from $57 billion to $133 billion.

The third leg of the debt problem, following consumer and business debt, is Uncle Sam. Government debt as of November 7, 2007, officially passed $9,000,000,000,000. That's about $30,000 for every man, woman, and child in the country. This total includes debt owned by many types of investors, from individuals to corporations to Federal Reserve banks and especially to foreign interests. (By 2004, foreign central banks had stockpiled more than $1.3 trillion worth of dollar-denominated Treasury bonds and agency bonds at the Federal Reserve. By 2007, foreign debt had nearly doubled, to $2.033 trillion.) What the $7.8 trillion figure does not account for are items like the gap between the government's Social Security and Medicare commitments and the money put aside to pay for them. If these items are factored in, the government debt burden for every American rises to well over $175,000.

In 2005, the Methuselah of investment mavens, Sir John Templeton, then 93, said you should get out of U.S. stocks, the U.S. dollar, and excess residential real estate. Templeton believed the dollar would fall 40 percent against other major currencies, and that this would lead the nation's major creditors—notably Japan and China—to dump their U.S. bonds, which would cause interest rates to run up, thus beginning a long period of stagflation. He was right.

Don't let his age fool you—Templeton was still sharp in 1999 when the financial industry hacks in Florida were urging their customers to buy more tech stocks. Templeton warned that the bubble would soon burst. He was right; they were wrong. Of course, he was only 87 back then. He is almost certainly right again.

Other great investors, too, are getting out of the dollar. For the first time in his life, Warren Buffett is investing in foreign currencies. George Soros, who made a fortune selling sterling in the 1992 ERM crisis, warns that the U.S. system could "blow up" at any time. Richard Russell, the influential editor of the *Dow Theory* letters, speaking at the New Orleans Investment Conference, warned: "If ever there was a crisis that could shake the global economy—this is it." Jim Rogers is teaching his daughter to speak Chinese.

When old-timers nod their heads in agreement—especially when they happen to be the most successful investors in the world—their advice may be worth listening to.

American consumers, companies, the U.S. government, and the country as a whole owe more dollars to more people than ever before. But perhaps the greatest threat to the U.S. economy is its foreign creditors. There is—or should be—a limit to the number of dollars foreigners are willing to buy and hold and thus a limit to their willingness to service our credit habit. Why? Because the United States, while still the world's number-one economic power, is showing itself to be an unreliable steward of its own currency.

Seeking to spur the economy to growth, the Fed and the Treasury have been actively devaluing the dollar. Many dubious excuses are given—protecting American exports, saving jobs, preventing deflation, for instance—but there is no question that Capitol Hill is actively engineering the dollar's demise: 18 rate cuts since 2001, three tax cuts, massive deficits, and record money creation bear cold witness to its manipulations.

You don't spend your way to prosperity; no nation ever has or ever will. But guess what? That very idea *is* the basis of U.S. and Fed monetary policy.

Never in U.S. history have the imbalances in the economy been so pronounced, or so dangerous. "My experience as an emerging markets analyst in the 1990s taught me to be on the lookout for signs of financial vulnerability," observed analyst Hernando Cortina in a Morgan Stanley research note.

> [The signs] include ballooning current-account and fiscal deficits, overvalued currencies, dependence on foreign portfolio flows, optimistic stock market valuations coupled with murky earnings, questionable corporate governance, and acrimonious political landscapes. Any one of these signals in an emerging market usually raises a red flag, and a market that combines all of them is almost surely best avoided or at least underweighted. I didn't imagine back then that one day these indicators would all be flashing red for the world's biggest and most important market—the U.S. A by-the-numbers analysis of America's macro accounts in a global context doesn't paint a flattering picture.[9]

Yet for growth-starved financial markets, perceptions and hope are often more important than economic reality. According to the macro indicators that the International Monetary Fund (IMF) uses to assess emerging-market economies, the United States fell between Turkey and Brazil.

Hernando Cortina politely concluded: "Investors contemplating the purchase of U.S. dollar-denominated assets would be wise to factor in significant dollar depreciation over the next few years."

"Households have been on a borrowing spree," added Northern Trust economist Asha Bangalore.

> Household borrowing as a percentage of disposable personal income hit a new high of 12.4 percent in the second quarter of 2003. This measure of household borrowing reflects mortgage borrowing, credit card borrowing, borrowing from banks, and the like. Household borrowing is not only at a record high but a new aspect has emerged—household borrowing advanced during the recession unlike in every other postwar recession when households reduced borrowing. The good news is that consumer demand continues to advance with the support from borrowing.[10]

The bad news is that no economy has ever borrowed its way to prosperity. Despite the conspiracy against it, the dollar has avoided a downright free fall. That's because dollar investors across the globe are still convinced that, given favorable credit conditions, the U.S. economy will surely reenter the heyday of the late 1990s, taking dollar-denominated assets to new heights. But someday soon, we think, investors will be disabused of their illusions. Sure, the stock market rallied briskly in the recent past, but the U.S. economy continues to struggle. Unemployment persists. And the twin deficits loom larger and larger.

If and when America's creditors—domestic and foreign—decide the country's massive, record-breaking level of debt is reason enough to get out of their dollar investments, the dollar will have nowhere to go but down, precipitously. We don't know when the exact moment of truth will arrive, but we know it cannot be far off.

Excessive debt is not the only ominous development in the U.S. economy. Just as foreboding is the American consumers' persistent belief that they are wealthier than they actually are. U.S. financial assets are, once again, in the grip of a large bubble. Take stocks, for instance: It may not be 1999, but investors are sure partying as if it were. If the S&P 500—an index made up of the country's largest companies—were to trade at its historical fair value, or at a price-earnings (P/E) ratio of 15, it would have to decline by 50 percent off its high. But bull markets don't typically start at fair value. If a new bull market were really starting—and stocks were actually undervalued—the S&P would be trading 67 percent lower, at a P/E of 10. But it's been so long since investors have seen P/E ratios in this range, they seem to believe stocks will never descend from their lofty heights.

The U.S. stock market is once again in the grip of a bubble. The Fed's frantic reflation campaign, government's tax cuts, and easy credit have worked their way into stocks, causing the market to burgeon and billow outward in a way completely dissociated from any real measure of value.

In fact, the rally in stocks has been so strong that it has rekindled investors' belief in a new bull market, full economic recovery in the United States, and a return to the glory days of the 1990s. But a funny thing has started to happen. The U.S. stock market is soaring. Normally, that means the dollar would go with it; when a country's stock market goes up, demand for its financial assets usually goes up, too. But the dollar is being dragged down by debt—government debt, personal debt, and corporate debt. Investors want a bull market, and so they're making one. But the dollar reflects the real state of the American economy . . . and it knows better.

Foreign investors are especially burned when stocks and the dollar part company. At first blush, the rallying U.S. stock market seems like a very inviting place for their capital. All denominations are welcome, but not all guests are treated equally well. For example, the S&P 500 soared 26.4 percent in 2004, in U.S. dollar terms. Yet euro-based investors in U.S. stocks would have realized only a 6 percent gain for the year.

Foreign bondholders are faring no better. Foreign central bank holdings of Treasury and agency securities total over $1 trillion. So, roughly speaking, every 10 percent drop in the dollar's value impoverishes our foreign creditors by about $100 billion on their U.S. Treasury holdings alone!

That's real money.

How is it possible that stocks continue their winning ways, even while the dollar continues its losing ways? These two inimical trends are strange bedfellows indeed.

What makes the pairing particularly bizarre is the fact that our nation relies so heavily upon the enthusiasm of foreign investors for U.S. assets.

What is the Fed doing, and why? One writer has pegged the answer:

> The Federal Reserve Board is working to raise the inflation rate, while the U.S. Treasury is trying to talk down the dollar exchange rate. Not every day does the world's hegemonic power pursue a policy of currency debasement. Still less frequently does it have the courtesy to tell its creditors what it's doing to them.[11]

Indeed. The Fed and Treasury are engaged in a kind of collusion to lower the dollar's value. And that's a very dangerous game to play, especially for a country like the United States, which relies so heavily upon foreign capital to finance its economy. It has become fashionable in the corridors of power in Washington to advocate "market-based" exchange rates—code for "weak dollar." A weak dollar, it is widely believed, will lead to a strong economy. Hmm.

In the olden days, of course, the Fed was supposed to pursue "monetary stability." But in the enlightened twenty-first century, the Fed has much grander designs. It imagines itself a kind of marionette master to the world's largest economy, making it dance whenever it wishes, simply by tugging on one little interest rate, or by tugging on the dollar. And so it tugs, and tugs, hoping to revive the economy.

The U.S. Treasury Department is also conspiring with the Fed to weaken the dollar. Hasn't Treasury Secretary Snow touted the weak dollar as a surefire cure for the struggling U.S. manufacturing sector? And hasn't the dollar been tumbling? And yet, isn't the manufacturing sector struggling just as much as it was when the price of a euro was only 83 cents, instead of $1.25?

It's obvious to almost every citizen who does not live in Washington, D.C., that devaluing the dollar to stimulate economic growth is a fool's mission. A couple of years ago, 255 dollar bills purchased one ounce of gold. Today, an ounce of gold costs more than

400 dollar bills. And on the day that an ounce of gold costs 1,000 dollar bills, our manufacturers will have become so competitive that they will be exporting firecrackers to the Chinese, or so the gang on Capitol Hill believes. But in fact, we will all be poorer for embracing the idiocy of "competitive devaluations." The problem is, once a devaluation trend begins, it is almost impossible to stop.

The solution comes from repositioning, and the best cues for when, how, and where are found in the gold market—which prospers during times of geopolitical uncertainty and traditionally rises in value when the dollar falls. The gold price has jumped 367 percent from April 2001 to January 2008, from $255 to $936. The metal's impressive rise inspired a dramatic rally in gold shares that has vaulted the XAU Index of gold stocks to an all-time high of $197.3 on January 14, 2008.

What does the gold market know? That the Fed's reflation campaign will succeed too well? A little bit of inflation—like a little wildfire—is a difficult thing to contain. And the gold market seems to have caught a whiff of inflationary smoke.

Or does the gold market know that Iraq will continue to serve as a breeding ground for terrorists and a habitat for anti-American terrorist acts? As the Iraq situation continues, the dollar will suffer . . . a lot.

Or maybe the gold market knows only that U.S. financial assets are very expensive, and worries, therefore, that U.S. stocks selling for 35 times earnings and U.S. bonds yielding 4.5 percent are all too pricey for risk-averse investors to own in large quantities. A vicious cycle is hard to stop. The dollar's descent is the most worrisome—and influential—trend in the financial markets today. And yet, as long as Cisco is "breaking out to the upside," few investors seem to care about the dollar's slide into the dustbin of monetary history. The dollar's demise is not inevitable, just highly likely.

When a currency falls, in theory anyway, interest rates usually rise. A government whose currency is falling apart tries to make assets denominated in that currency more attractive by paying higher rates of interest to potential investors. And if the government doesn't raise rates, the market will do it by selling off bonds and driving yields up.

And so, in theory, you would normally expect to see a falling U.S. dollar accompanied by rising U.S. interest rates. The difficulty from the Bush/Greenspan/Bernanke perspective is that rising long-term rates pose an enormous problem: They make it significantly more expensive for debtors—from U.S. consumers to the U.S. government—to service their obligations. And these costs are not negligible.

In fiscal year 2007, for example, the government was obliged to pay out a whopping $429 billion in interest expense on the public debt outstanding. At a 1 percent rise in interest rates, that would add $43 billion in interest expense. And to meet this added interest expense, the government would, of course, have to float even more bonds, and at the higher interest rate.

This scenario is the government's nightmare. When the falling dollar eventually pushes interest rates up, the Treasury will have to issue more debt at higher interest rates simply to pay off its existing debt. But if the Asian economic juggernaut were to discontinue recycling its excess dollars into U.S. government bonds and Fannie Mae debt, the dollar would suffer mightily. How much longer until our luck runs out?

In some way, shape, or form foreigners lend our consumption-crazed nation $1 trillion every year. We Americans, in turn, use the money they send our way to buy SUVs, plasma TVs, and costly military campaigns in distant lands. However, we do not forget to repay our creditors with ever-cheaper dollars. Someday soon, foreigners must lose interest in subsidizing our consumption habit.

That the dollar's decline comes at the urging of the same nation that prints the things is an irony that is not lost on the world's largest dollar holders. Reading the tea leaves, many Asian central banks are still exploring ways to lighten up on their U.S. dollar holdings. "The Chinese aren't lapping up our Treasury paper for its great investment attributes," writes Stephanie Pomboy of MacroMavens, "but [rather] because of a mechanical need to maintain the yuan/dollar peg."[12]

The dollar is a currency fated to tumble. The dollar's resistance to its debt load, fueled by the machinations of central banks and the misguided faith of dollar investors, undoubtedly qualifies as a trend whose premise is false. Sometime soon this trend will be discredited.

Fortunately, there are many ways you can capitalize on a falling dollar. From the wide range of possibilities, four investment strategies follow, each designed to suit a variety of investing styles. Using one or several of these recommendations, you can craft a personalized plan of action.

Direct Short-Term Speculation: Dollar Index Put Options

The most direct—albeit short-term—approach to betting against the dollar is to buy put options on Dollar Index futures. The U.S. Dollar Index (USDX) trades on the New York Board of Trade under the symbol DX. The USDX was invented in 1973—ironically, two years after Nixon closed the gold window, and the same year the gold standard was completely abandoned. Using a base of 100, the USDX measures the market value of the dollar versus the trade-weighted geometric average of six currencies (although 17 countries are represented in the index because there are 15 countries that use the euro). The six currencies are the euro, the Japanese yen, the U.K. pound, the Canadian dollar, the Swedish krona, and the Swiss franc.

Why these countries and these currencies? These six currencies constitute most of America's international trade (excepting Mexico and China), and have relatively well-developed foreign exchange markets. Most important, the values of these currencies are, with the exception of central bank intervention, freely determined by market forces and market participants.

As you can see from the graph of the U.S. Dollar Index in Figure 8.2, the greenback has been in decline against a basket of currencies since the beginning of 2002. It was hovering around the 87 level by late 2004. Given the dollar's continuing predicament, we can see nowhere for it to go but down.

Purchasing put options on the USDX is the most direct way to capitalize on the dollar's decline. By purchasing these options, you'll be paying the price—known as the premium—to have the right for a fixed period of time *but not the obligation* to be short the Dollar Index at a specific level. Should the dollar fail to fall, or should it even rally (highly unlikely), you would simply not exercise your right to be short the dollar—forfeiting the premium paid for the put option, but no more.

Consider buying U.S. Dollar Index put options dated at least four months into the future, looking for the index to fall below 80. Your maximum risk is the price you pay for your options plus transaction costs. Your profit potential is unlimited.

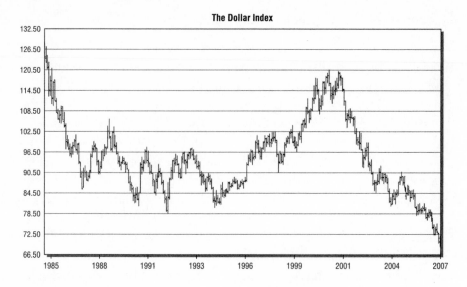

Figure 8.2 U.S. Dollar Index (USDX)

Direct Short-Term Speculation: Euro Call Options

Buying euro call options is almost identical to buying puts on the U.S. Dollar Index. If the dollar drops, the euro should rise. But whereas the Dollar Index measures the greenback's value against a basket of foreign currencies, the euro is only one of the currencies in the Dollar Index. Buying calls on the euro, therefore, is a more focused trade.

The euro boasts one very important virtue that the dollar lacks: a current account *surplus.* Because the euro bloc countries produce a current account surplus, there is an automatic, natural demand for euros. Conversely, America's large and growing current account deficit produces continuous selling pressure on the dollar.

Just as for the dollar puts, call options on euro currency futures are promising ways to sell the dollar. The euro index has been rising steadily since the dollar peaked in February of 2002. The futures market for euros will anticipate further upward movement, rewarding buyers of call options on the euro.

Consider buying Euro FX call options dated at least four months into the future. Your maximum risk is the price you pay for your options plus transaction costs. Your profit potential is unlimited.

Direct Long-Term Speculation: Foreign Currency Certificates of Deposit

For most investors, the surest way to profit from the weakening U.S. dollar is to invest directly in strong currencies and their certificates of deposit (CDs). By investing directly in a strong currency, you reduce your risks considerably because you are dealing with a single investment that you own outright and can easily monitor. At the same time, you can be certain to receive whatever exchange-rate advantages may develop between your foreign currency and the weakening U.S. dollar.

Until recently, opening a foreign currency account could be done only through an offshore bank. Many countries did not make it easy for their banks to deal with Americans. In addition, offshore bank accounts led to additional paperwork with the IRS and an increased chance for an audit. Fortunately for U.S. investors, foreign currency accounts are now easily available. For example, Everbank offers retail-oriented FDIC-insured deposit accounts and certificates of deposit denominated in any of the world's major currencies.

One of Everbank's most interesting CDs is the Commodity Index CD. Paying the highest interest rate of any world currency CD—with the exception of the Mexican peso and the South African rand—the Commodity Index CD is comprised of the Australian dollar, New Zealand dollar, Canadian dollar, and South African rand. These currencies are grouped together because their economies are all driven by commodities exports. China's economy will continue to grow sharply, leading to increased demand for commodities that Australia and New Zealand offer. A six-month Commodity Index CD yields 4.16 percent, as we go to press.

All-Season Dollar Hedge: Gold

Gold is the ultimate dollar hedge. It is the only global currency that is no one's liability. It is "pure money." As such, gold has always provided a kind of insurance, first and foremost. It is not an investment per se. But when economic uncertainties mount, buying a bit of gold "insurance" can be a terrific investment.

"If gold isn't a bargain, what is it? It is a hedge," says Jim Grant, editor of *Grant's Interest Rate Observer.* "However, in my opinion, it is a hedge bargain. The value of a hedge should vary according to the cost and evidence of the risks being hedged against. In the case of gold, the risks are monetary."

The abandonment of the gold standard in 1971 was a crucial turning point in the U.S. economy, a decision that has been gradually destroying the power of the United States. The excessive printing of currency led directly to the trade deficit, and once the surplus turned, it never went back. It aggravated the condition of the national debt and allowed the Fed unbridled access to printing presses, the condition in which we find ourselves today.

The lesson not yet learned has everything to do with the reasons why the gold standard was so important. We have given control of economic forces over to government tinkering. Ludwig von Mises, noted twentieth-century economist, was a believer in allowing market forces and not government to determine monetary policy:

> Mises argued that because money originated as a market commodity, not by government edict or social contract, it should be returned to the market. Banking should be treated as any other industry in a market economy, and be subject to competition.[13]

In one of his many writings, Mises correctly observed, "The significance of adherence to a metallic-money system lies in the freedom of the value of money from state influence that such a system guarantees."[14]

This is the crux of the monetary struggle of our era. With governments virtually off the gold standard, the market itself is not trusted to set the course of *value* in the exchange of goods and services. That is why, ultimately, the destruction of the dollar is inevitable. Governments—including the U.S. government along with the Fed—have not yet learned that the economy cannot be controlled. But as Mises explained, it is not just monetary policy but part of a larger social trend that has brought us to this moment:

> The struggle against gold which is one of the main concerns of all contemporary governments must not be looked upon as an isolated phenomenon. It is but one item in the gigantic process of destruction

which is the mark of our time. People fight the gold standard because they want to substitute national autarky for free trade, war for peace, totalitarian government omnipotence for liberty.[15]

If all of this is true—and from the economic news of the past few years, it appears so—what can you do to turn this situation into an advantage? The answer is to use free-market gold to exploit the market tendency of gold itself. Remember, even when governments are off the gold standard, the market for gold cannot be controlled. It is worth whatever people will pay. As long as you understand what causes the price of gold to move, you have the key to investing success. That key is:

The price of gold tends to move in a direction opposite the value of the dollar.

With this simple observation, we can track the value of gold and the value of the dollar together to see how they interact with one another. After 2000, the dollar fell and gold prices rose. As the dollar continues to fall, it makes sense that gold will move upward in direct response. We could explain this by noting that value itself is not created out of nothing; it simply changes hands. So as value goes out of the dollar, it can be measured by watching other currencies rise, but it can also be measured by watching gold prices move in the other direction opposite the dollar.

As the Fed continues to keep the printing presses running around the clock, the dollar continues to weaken. The problem is not entirely visible because, even with its gradual decline, the dollar has remained strong. This has been so partly because China's currency is largely pegged to the dollar, but also because in many respects, the United States continues to lead economically in the world. However, the trend in economic growth tells us that this cannot continue indefinitely. It is economic common sense that currencies tend to be the strongest for those nations with superior economic growth. If you understand why it is important to invest in gold as a defensive measure against the declining dollar, the next question is *where* to invest. You have many choices.

Five ways to invest in gold are explained in the following paragraphs. Based on your level of market experience and familiarity with products, one of these will be appropriate for you.

1. *Direct ownership.* There is nothing like gold bullion, the ultimate expression of pure value. Historically, many civilizations have recognized the permanence of gold's value. For example, Egyptian civilizations buried vast amounts of gold with deceased pharaohs in the belief that they would be able to use it in the afterlife. Great wars were fought, among other reasons, to pillage stores of gold. Why the allure? The answer: Gold is the only *real* money, and its value cannot be changed or controlled by government fiat—the underlying reason for governments to go off the gold standard, unfortunately. Gold's value will rise based on the pure forces of supply and demand, no matter what Mr. Bernanke decrees regarding interest rates or greenbacks in circulation.

The big disadvantage to owning gold is that it tends to trade with a wide spread between bid and ask prices. So don't expect to turn a fast profit. You'll buy at retail and sell at wholesale, so you'll need a big price jump just to break even. However, you should not view gold as a speculative asset, but a defensive asset for holding value. Since your dollars are going to fall in value, gold is the best place to preserve value. The best forms for gold ownership are through minted coins: one-ounce South African Krugerrands, Canadian Maple Leafs, or American Eagles.

2. *Gold exchange-traded funds.* The recent explosion in exchange-traded funds (ETFs) presents an even more interesting way to invest in gold. An ETF is a type of mutual fund that trades on a stock exchange like an ordinary stock. The ETF's exact portfolio is fixed in advance and does not change. Thus, the two gold ETFs that trade in the United States both hold gold bullion as their one and only asset. You can locate these two ETFs under the symbol "GLD" (for the streetTRACKS Gold Trust) and "IAU" (for the iShares COMEX Gold Trust). Either ETF offers a practical way to hold gold in an investment portfolio.

3. *Gold mutual funds.* For people who are hesitant to invest in physical gold, but still desire some exposure to the precious metal, gold mutual funds provide a helpful alternative. These funds hold portfolios of gold stocks—that is, the stocks of companies like Newmont Mining that mine for gold. Newmont is an example of a senior gold stock.

A senior is a large, well-capitalized company that has been around several years and has a profitable track record. They tend to own established mines that produce known quantities of gold each year. For many investors, selection of such a company is a more moderate or conservative play (versus picking up cheap shares in fairly young companies).

4. *Junior gold stocks.* This level of stock is more speculative. Junior stocks are less likely to own productive mines, and may be exploration plays—with higher potential profits but also with greater risk of loss. Capitalization is likely to be smaller than capitalization of the senior gold stocks. This range of investments is for investors whose risk tolerance is broader, and who accept the possibility of gold-based losses in exchange for the potential for triple-digit gains.

5. *Gold options and futures.* For the more sophisticated and experienced investor, options allow you to speculate on gold prices. In the options market, you can speculate on price movements in either direction. If you buy a call, you are hoping prices will rise. A call fixes the purchase price so the higher that price goes, the greater the margin between your fixed option price and current market price. When you buy a put, you expect the price to fall. Buying options is risky, and more people lose than win. In fact, about three-fourths of all options bought expire worthless. The options market is complex and requires experience and understanding.

To generalize, options possess two key traits—one bad and one good. The good trait is that they enable an investor to control a large investment with a small, and limited, amount of money. The bad trait is that options expire within a fixed period of time. Thus, for the buyer time is the enemy because as the expiration date gets closer, an option's time value disappears. Anyone investing in options needs to understand all of the risks before spending money.

The futures market is far too complex for the vast majority of investors. Even experienced options investors recognize the high-risk nature of the futures market. Considering the range of ways to get into the gold market, futures trading is the most complex and, while big fortunes could be made, they can also be lost in an instant.

We cannot know, predict, or even guess *when* the demise of the dollar is going to occur, or how quickly it will take place. But we do know it is going to occur. The tragic mismanagement of monetary policy by the Fed over many years has made this inevitable.

Removing the U.S. monetary system from the gold standard was not merely a decision of short-term effect. Nixon may have seen the move as a means for solving current economic problems, but it had long-lasting impacts: trade deficits, growing federal debt, and the ability to print money endlessly and build a new credit-based economy. Internationally, the decision by the United States virtually forced all other major currencies to also go off the gold standard.

Any investor who views the economic situation broadly—both domestically and internationally—can see that trouble lies ahead. We have delayed the inevitable because China is a partner in our monetary woes. The Chinese are building their own debt on the dubious foundation of the U.S. dollar, and other Asian economies have been forced to go along for the ride. When the dollar falls, many other countries will suffer as well. The offset, logically, is found in commodities. Investing in oil stocks makes sense, for example, because the price of oil is rising and as it becomes more difficult to drill oil those companies that own drilling and exploration operations will benefit. It makes sense to invest in other commodities as well. The *tangible* asset play is clearly where future value is going to lie. With China's never-ending need for coal, iron ore, tungsten, copper, oil, and other metals, the future of tangible markets is the bright spot in the gloomy financially based economics of the world.

Leading the charge is gold. It is ironic that monetary policy follows a predictable pattern. Governments overprint money and their currency crashes. Inevitably, they always return to gold, but often at great expense and with considerable suffering. We find ourselves in another one of those moments in time where irresponsible monetary policy has put us at risk. But we don't have to simply hold on and wait for the demise of the dollar; we can take action now because that demise *is* great for your portfolio—if you position yourself in tangible assets rather than in empty fiat promises and the bizarre economic premise of U.S. monetary policy.

Remember the observation we made earlier: Goods and services can be paid for only with goods and services. Currency is nothing but an IOU, a promissory note that is *not* backed up with any tangible value. Once we reach our national credit limit, monetary policy will be forced to retreat. When that happens, traditional investors and their savings accounts are going to be hit hard. The beneficiary of the falling dollar will be the investor whose holdings emphasize tangible value of goods: resources and precious metals.

Every danger to one group of people is invariably an opportunity to another. It all depends on where you position yourself. Those investors positioned in dollar-based investments are going to suffer the loss of purchasing power when the dollar's value disappears. Those who moved their investments to higher ground will benefit from the change.

NOTES

INTRODUCTION: FALL OF THE GREAT DOLLAR STANDARD

1. J. N. Tlaga, "How the Fiat Money Is Being Defended," at www.gold-eagle.com.
2. Fed Chairman Arthur Burns, quoted in *The Commanding Heights: The Battle for the World Economy,* by Daniel Yergin and Joseph Stanislaw (New York: Free Press, revised and updated edition, 2002).
3. Today the IMF has 184 member countries. Its objective is to work for international monetary stability and promote trade (web site: www.imf.org).
4. The World Bank describes its mission: "It is a development Bank which provides loans, policy advice, technical assistance and knowledge sharing services to low and middle income countries to reduce poverty." Web site: www.worldbank.org.
5. Pamphlet, *Pillars of Peace,* May 1946, Book Department of the Army Information School.

CHAPTER 1: THE RECOVERY THAT WASN'T

1. David Walker, Letter, "Report to the Secretary of the Treasury," Financial Audit, Bureau of the Public Debt's Fiscal Years 2007 and 2006 Schedules of Federal Debt, November 2007.

2. Ibid.
3. "Our Nation's Fiscal Outlook: The Federal Government's Long-Term Budget Imbalance," at www.gao.gov/special.pubs/longterm.
4. Alan Greenspan from Congressional testimony on July 17, 2002.
5. www.federalreserve.gov/Releses?G19/Current.
6. "Fiscal Fitness: The U.S. Budget Deficit's Uncertain Prospects,"*Economic Letter—Insights* 2, no. 4, April 2007, Federal Reserve Bank of Dallas.

CHAPTER 2: FICTITIOUS CAPITALISM AND THE iPOD ECONOMY

1. *BusinessWeek,* October 27, 2003.
2. To view recent NIPA data, check the BEA web site at www.bea.doc.gov/bea/dn/nipaweb/SelectTable.asp?Selected=Y.

CHAPTER 3: PATHOLOGICAL CONSUMPTION

1. The term *conspicuous consumption* was coined by Thorstein Veblen in *The Theory of the Leisure Class* (1899). Also called "pathological purchasing," it refers to the tendency by individuals or society as a whole to consume to excess.
2. Joan Robinson, "Reconsideration of the Theory of Free Trade,"*Collected Economic Papers,* Volume IV, 1973.
3. Alain René Lesage, *Gil Blas,* 1735.
4. John C. Edmunds, "Securities: The New World Wealth Machine,"*Foreign Policy,* Fall 1996, at www.foreignpolicy.com.
5. The Institute for Supply Management publishes the index as a means for monitoring trends in the industry. Web site: www.ism.ws/AboutISM/index.cfm.
6. See "Haute Con Job," PIMCO *Investment Outlook,* October 2004.
7. The G-5 nations are the United States, United Kingdom, France, Germany, and Japan.
8. Warren Buffett, Letter to the Shareholders of Berkshire Hathaway, 2006.
9. Warren Buffett, "America's Growing Trade Deficit Is Selling the Nation Out from under Us,"*Fortune,* October 2003.

CHAPTER 4: SHORT UNHAPPY EPISODES IN MONETARY HISTORY

1. Emergency Banking Relief Act of 1933.
2. "The Trader" column in *Barron's,* March 27, 1933.
3. Ibid., March 13, 1933.

4. Marco Polo and Ronald Latham, *The Travels of Marco Polo,* Penguin, reissued edition, 1958.

5. John Law, quoted in "How John Law's Failed Experiment Gave Us a New Word: Millionaire," at www.freepublic.com.

6. Ibid.

7. Byron King, "Making Money in Early America,"*The Daily Reckoning,* December 12, 2004.

8. H. A. Scott Trask, "Inflation and the American Revolution," Mises Organization at www.mises.org, July 18, 2003.

9. John Mackay, in Foreword to Andrew Dickson White, *Fiat Money in France: How It Came, What It Brought, and How It Ended* (Caldwell, ID: Caxton Printers Ltd., 1972; reprint of 1914 original edition).

10. Charles A. Coombs, *The Arena of International Finance* (New York: John Wiley & Sons, 1976).

11. Cordell Hull, *The Memoirs of Cordell Hull* (New York: Macmillan, 1948).

12. Harry Dexter White, quoted in Robert A. Pollard, *Economic Security and the Origins of the Cold War, 1945–1950* (New York: Columbia University Press, 1985).

13. Wikipedia, at http://en.wikipedia.org.

14. Ibid.

15. John Maynard Keynes, speech at the closing plenary session, Bretton Woods Conference, July 22, 1944; in Donald Moggeridge, ed., *The Collected Writings of John Maynard Keynes* (London: Cambridge University Press, 1980).

16. Secretary of State George Marshall, speech, "Against Hunger, Poverty, Desperation and Chaos," Harvard University commencement address, June 1947.

17. Cited in Francis J. Gavin, *Gold, Dollars and Power: The Politics of International Monetary Relations, 1958–1971* (Chapel Hill: University of North Carolina Press, 2003).

18. Barry Eichengreen, *Golden Fetters: The Gold Standard and the Great Depression 1919–1939* (New York: Oxford University Press, 1992).

19. Clif Droke, "Paper Money in the Balance,"*Gold Digest,* December 13, 2002.

20. Gerald P. Dwyer Jr. and James R. Lothian, "International Money and Common Obstacles in Historical Perspective," at www.independent.org, May 2002.

21. Robert S. Lopez, "The Dollar of the Middle Ages," *Journal of Economic History,* Summer 1951.

22. Nathan Sussman, "Debasements, Royal Revenues, and Inflation in France during the Hundred Years' War," *Journal of Economic History,* March 1993.

23. Peter Spufford, "Le role de la monnaie dans le révolution commerciale du XIII siècle," in *Etudes d'historie monétaire,* Lille, France: Presses universitaires de Lille, 1984.

24. J. M. Cipolla, *Money, Prices, and Civilization in the Mediterranean World, Fifth to Seventeenth Century* (New York: St. Martin's Press, 1967).

25. Dwyer and Lothian, "International Money."
26. David Walker, Letter, "Report to the Secretary of the Treasury," Financial Audit, Bureau of the Public Debt's Fiscal Years 2007 and 2006 Schedules of Federal Debt, November 2007.
27. Kevin Down, "The Emergence of Fiat Money: A Reconsideration," *Cato Journal,* Winter 2001.
28. Lawrence Parks, "What the President Should Know about Our Monetary System," at www.fame.org, September 12, 1999.
29. Franklin D. Roosevelt, radio address, March 10, 1933.
30. Richard Duncan, *The Dollar Crisis* (Hoboken, NJ: John Wiley & Sons, 2003).
31. Ludwig von Mises, *The Theory of Money and Credit* (Indianapolis, IN: Liberty Fund, 1980).
32. Ibid.
33. Jeffrey M. Herbener, "Ludwig von Mises on the Gold Standard and Free Banking," *Quarterly Journal of Austrian Economics,* Spring 2002.
34. Ibid.

CHAPTER 5: THE HELICOPTER THEORY, INFLATION, AND THE MONEY IN YOUR WALLET

1. This section is based on Dr. Kurt Richebächer's "The Austrian Case against American Monetarism," *The Daily Reckoning,* June 7, 2000.
2. www.oecd.org.
3. This section and the remainder of this chapter are based on material in "Doomsday for the Dollar," Special Report, *Richebšcher Letter,* 2003.
4. *BusinessWeek Online,* 2002 S&P Core Earnings table.
5. Janice Revell, "CEO Pensions: The Latest Way to Hide Millions," *Fortune,* April 28, 2003.
6. Ben S. Bernanke, "National and Regional Economic Overview," Charlotte Chamber of Commerce, Charlotte, North Carolina, November 29, 2007.
7. Ibid.
8. Ibid.
9. Ibid.

CHAPTER 6: ATTENTION TO DEFICITS DISORDER

1. H. A. Scott Trask, "Perpetual Debt: From the British Empire to the American Hegamon," at www.mises.org, January 27, 2004.
2. Ibid.
3. Ibid.

4. David Walker, Letter, "Report to the Secretary of the Treasury," Financial Audit, Bureau of the Public Debt's Fiscal Years 2007 and 2006 Schedules of Federal Debt, November 2007.

5. Jon Dougherty, "Is the United States Flat-Out Broke?" *World Net-Daily,* June 6, 2003.

6. Hans F. Sennholz, "The Surplus Hoax," at www.mises.org, November 3, 2000.

7. www.cbo.gov.

8. In *The Birds* (play by Aristophanes, ca. 415 B.C.), Cloud Cuckoo Land was a utopian land existing in the air between heaven and earth, where everything was perfect and all problems solved themselves.

9. Cited in Murray N. Rothbard, "Repudiating the National Debt," at www.mises.org, January 16, 2004.

10. Adam Smith, *The Wealth of Nations,* 1776.

11. "A national debt, if it is not excessive, will be to us a national blessing."—Alexander Hamilton, in a letter dated April 30, 1781.

12. Joseph Kennedy II, quoted in *Newsweek,* February 9, 1967.

13. Joint Economic Committee, United States Congress: "Deficits, Taxation, and Spending," April 2003; and "Hidden Costs of Government Spending," staff report, 2001.

14. Joint Economic Committee, "Deficits, Taxation, and Spending."

15. Joint Economic Committee, United States Congress: James Gwartney, Robert Lawson, and Randall Holcombe, "The Size and Functions of Government and Economic Growth," 1998.

16. Senator John C. Calhoun (Democratic-Republican Party, South Carolina), speech, August 5, 1842.

17. Gerald W. Scully, "Measuring the Burden of High Taxes," Policy Report No. 215, National Center for Policy Analysis, July 1998.

18. International Monetary Fund, "Global Financial Market Developments."

19. Peter Warburton, *Debt and Delusion: Central Bank Follies That Threaten Economic Disaster,* 2nd ed. (London: Penguin Books, 2000).

20. Alan Greenspan, testimony before the Committee on Banking, Housing, and Urban Affairs, February 17, 2005.

21. "Real" GDP is the total value of activity at price levels for the year. The importance of this measurement is that it tracks changes in purchasing power from one year to the next. In the usual measurement of GDP, the trend is distorted because inflation isn't adjusted, so reduced value in the U.S. dollar can make GDP look far different than the real numbers.

22. Catherine L. Mann, "Is the U.S. Current Account Deficit Sustainable?" *Finance and Development,* IMF, March 2000.

23. Edwin M. Truman (Institute for International Economics), "The U.S. Current Account Deficit and the Euro Area," speech at the "ECB and Its Watchers" Conference, Frankfurt, Germany, July 2, 2004.

CHAPTER 7:   ALAS, THE DEMISE OF THE DOLLAR

1. Marc Faber, *Tomorrow's Gold* (Hong Kong: CLSA Books, 2003).
2. "Historical Statistics of the United States," at www2.census.gov/prod2/statcomp/documents/CT1970p1-01.pdf.
3. *Brenner's Prophecies,* Washington, D.C., 1884.
4. Cesar Bacani, *The China Investor* (Hoboken, NJ: John Wiley & Sons, 2002).
5. John W. Wheeler-Bennett, *The Nemesis of Power* (New York: Macmillan, 1953).
6. Richard Daughty, "A Financial Fiasco," *The Daily Reckoning,* November 24, 2004.
7. Ben Bernanke, "The Chinese Economy: Progress and Challenges," remarks at the Chinese Academy of Social Sciences, Beijing, China, December 15, 2006.
8. Eric J. Fry, "Salvation by Devaluation," *The Daily Reckoning,* January 19, 2004.
9. "Greenspan Sees 'Little' Trouble in Global Current Account Adjustment," press briefing, U.S. Consulate, January 13, 2004, at http://mumbai.usconsulate.gov.
10. Alan Greenspan, remarks at the Bundesbank, Berlin, Germany, January 13, 2004.
11. Adam Smith, *The Wealth of Nations,* 1776.
12. Alan Greenspan, Adam Smith Memorial Lecture, Fife College in Kirkcaldy, Fife, Scotland, February 6, 2005.
13. Alan Greenspan, remarks at the Bundesbank, Berlin, Germany, January 13, 2004.
14. Ibid.
15. Ibid.
16. Ibid.
17. 1923 Deutsches Reich postage, Scott catalog stamp No. 270.
18. William Meyer, "Warren Buffett's Economic and Political Influence Grows Each Year," *Personal Finance,* May 29, 2004, at www.persfin.co.za.
19. Robert Lenzner and Daniel Kruger, "A Word from a Dollar Bear," *Forbes,* January 10, 2005, at www.forbes.com.
20. "Federal Reserve," Wikipedia, at http://en.wikipedia.org.
21. Milton Friedman and Anna J. Schwartz, *A Monetary History of the United States, 1867–1960* (Princeton, NJ: Princeton University Press, 1971).

CHAPTER 8:   CRISIS AND OPPORTUNITY IN THE TWILIGHT OF THE GREAT DOLLAR STANDARD ERA

1. "America Betrayed," Special Report, *Strategic Investment,* 2004.
2. Marc Faber, *Tomorrow's Gold* (Hong Kong: CLSA Books, 2003).

3. The mythological power accumulated by Damocles led to him being punished by the tyrant Dionysius I. To teach his rival a lesson, Dionysius I ordered that a sword was to be placed above Damocles' head suspended by a single hair. Because the hair could snap at any time, references to "the sword of Damocles" have come to mean any situation characterized by an ever-present danger.

4. Kevin Kerr, "The New Oil Crisis Has Arrived! Are You Ready for $100 per Barrel?" *Outstanding Investments,* November 2004.

5. Sean Corrigan, London correspondent for *The Daily Reckoning,* 2004.

6. Jim Rogers, Essay 12, *The Daily Reckoning,* March 13, 2003.

7. Marc Faber, "The Gloom, Boom, Doom Report," November 2003, at www.gloomboomdoom.com.

8. David Rosenberg, *CNN Money,* October 3, 2003.

9. Hernando Cortina, Morgan Stanley research note.

10. Asha Bangalore, at www.northerntrust.com, September 19, 2003.

11. James Grant, "The Dollar Meltdown," *Forbes,* October 13, 2003.

12. Stephanie Pomboy, quoted in *The Daily Reckoning,* September 23, 2003.

13. Biography of Ludwig von Mises at www.mises.org.

14. Ludwig von Mises, "Monetary Stabilization and Cyclical Policy," in *On Manipulation of Money and Credit* (Dobbs Ferry, NY: Free Market Books, 1978).

15. Ludwig von Mises, *Human Action: A Treatise on Economics* (Auburn, AL: Ludwig von Mises Institute, 1998).

INDEX

The Demise of the Dollar...
And Why It's Even Better for Your Investments

As the dollar continues its downward spiral, investors need to take a critical look at where they put their hard-earned money. Regardless of what happens with the economy, you can make solid returns in the stock market, provided you know where to look. That's why we're offering you two additional bonus gifts that will help you navigate your way through today's market.

Bonus #1: *Fiat Currency: Using the Past to See Into the Future*

Inside this free report, you'll gain a thorough understanding of the fiat currency and how to capitalize on the greatest surge in gold prices in market history. Plus, we'll give you five entirely new ways to play gold's powerful rise.

All the details will be revealed in your special bonus report.

Bonus #2: *A free subscription to Agora Financial's* **5 Min. Forecast**

The 5 Min. Forecast is a premier e-letter brought to you by Agora Financial. *The 5 Min. Forecast* is full of quick, lucid, and compelling thoughts from Agora Financial's editors and analysts.

Delivered to your inbox daily, *The 5*'s quick-hitting news flash provides you with a fresh perspective on the markets and plenty of entertainment.

One loyal reader says…

"The 5 is No. 1 to read versus all other media I use. It says more in five minutes than any other media, and it's perfect for an overview of whatever I need to know. You're the best."

Another reader tells us…

"Your 5 Min. Forecast has become my favorite financial newsletter out of about 20 different ones I receive on a mostly daily basis. Putting it another way, I would give up the entire other 19 before I would give up this one."

Don't miss out on what another reader describes as…

"Great — incisive, quick and dirty and witty — 5 Min. summaries!"

To claim your special report and accept your free subscription to *The 5 Min. Forecast,* simply visit, http://www.agorafinancialpublications.com/Reports/Fiat.html